The Modern Language Association of America

Selected Bibliographies in Language and Literature

Walter S. Achtert, Series Editor

1. Roger D. Lund. *Restoration and Early Eighteenth-Century English Literature, 1660–1740: A Selected Bibliography of Resource Materials.* 1980.

2. Richard Kempton. *French Literature: An Annotated Guide to Selected Bibliographies.* 1981.

3. William A. Wortman. *A Guide to Serial Bibliographies for Modern Literatures.* 1982.

4. Hensley C. Woodbridge. *Spanish and Spanish-American Literature: An Annotated Guide to Selected Bibliographies.* 1983.

5. Hensley C. Woodbridge. *Guide to Reference Works for the Study of the Spanish Language and Literature and Spanish American Literature.* 1987.

6. Bobby J. Chamberlain. *Portuguese Language and Luso-Brazilian Literature: An Annotated Guide to Selected Reference Works.* 1989.

Portuguese Language and Luso-Brazilian Literature

An Annotated Guide to Selected Reference Works

Bobby J. Chamberlain

The Modern Language Association of America
New York, New York   1989

PC
5041
.Z9
C45
1989

Copyright © 1989 by The Modern Language Association of America

Library of Congress Cataloging-in-Publication Data

Chamberlain, Bobby J.
    Portuguese language and Luso-Brazilian literature: an annotated guide to
selected reference works / Bobby J. Chamberlain.
        p.   cm. — (Selected bibliographies in language and literature; 6)
    Includes index.
    ISBN 0-87352-956-1
    ISBN 0-87352-957-X (pbk.)
    1. Reference works — Portuguese philology — Bibliography. 2. Portuguese
philology — Bibliography. I. Title. II. Series.
Z2725.A2C45 1989
[PC5041]
016.869 — dc19   88-8409

Published by The Modern Language Association of America
10 Astor Place, New York, New York 10003-6981

Contents

Introduction   ix

Portuguese Language and Linguistics

Bibliographies, Indexes, Catalogs, Guides, Directories, and Manuals of
    Works on the Portuguese of Portugal and Brazil   3
Etymological Dictionaries   9
Historical Dictionaries   10
Dictionaries of Modern Portuguese   11
Synonyms and Antonyms   14
Bilingual Dictionaries   15
Word Formation   16
Onomastics   16
Encyclopedias   16
Dictionaries of Popular Expressions, Regionalisms, and Argot
  Portugal   18
  Brazil
    General   19
    Southeast   22
    South   22
    Northeast   23
    North   24
    West-Central   24
  Other Portuguese-Speaking Areas
    Macao   25
    Mozambique   25
    Madeira   25

Portuguese Literature

Current Bibliographies and Periodical Indexes   29
General Reference Works
  Bibliographies   29
  Dictionaries of Authors and Biobibliographies   30
  Genres
    Theater   32
Reference Works Dealing with Particular Periods, Authors, or Works
  Middle Ages
    General   33
    Festschriften Index   34

Arthurian Legends	34
Ballads	34
Galician-Portuguese Poetry	34
Cantigas d'escárnio e maldizer	35
A demanda do Santo Graal	35
Authors	35
Classical Period	
General Bibliographies and Library Catalogs	36
Sermons	36
Authors	36
Eighteenth Century	
Folhetos	37
Nineteenth Century	
General Bibliography	38
Authors	38
Twentieth Century	
Authors	39
Stylistics	40
Bibliographies of Translations	
General	40
Portugal	41
Comparative Literature and Cross-Cultural Scholarship	
General	42
Portugal	42
Bibliographies of Dissertations	
United States	
General	42
Hispanic and Luso-Brazilian	43
Western Europe	44
France	44
Germany and Austria	44
United Kingdom and Ireland	45
National Bibliographies	45
Union Lists and Library and Collection Catalogs	
General	
United States	46
France	46
Spain	47
United Kingdom	47
Portugal	
United States	48
Germany	49
Netherlands	49
United Kingdom	49

Bibliographies of Bibliographies   50

Brazilian Literature

Current Bibliographies and Periodical Indexes   53
Library and Resource Guides   54
General Reference Works
   Bibliographies   55
   Dictionaries of Literary Terms   58
   Dictionaries of Authors and Biobibliographies   58
   Genres
     Popular Poetry   61
     Poetry   61
     Theater   61
     Short Story and Novella   62
     Novel   63
     Folk Narrative   63
     Children's Literature   63
   States
     Maranhão   64
     Rio de Janeiro   64
     Rio Grande do Sul   64
     São Paulo   65
   Special Topics and Miscellaneous
     Criticism   65
     Afro-Brazilians   65
     Women   65
Reference Works Dealing with Particular Periods, Authors, or Works
   Colonial Period
     General   65
     Authors   66
   Nineteenth and Early Twentieth Centuries
     General   66
     Authors   66
   Modernism
     General   69
     Authors   69
Pseudonyms   72
Stylistics   72
Bibliographies of Translations
   General   72
   Latin America and Brazil   73
Comparative Literature and Cross-Cultural Scholarship
   General   75

Latin America and Brazil 75
Bibliographies of Dissertations
United States
  General 76
  Hispanic and Luso-Brazilian 76
  Brazil 77
  Western Europe 77
  France 77
  Germany and Austria 77
  United Kingdom and Ireland 78
National Bibliographies
  General Bibliographical Studies 78
  Brazilian Bibliographies 78
Union Lists and Library and Collection Catalogs
  General
    United States 79
    France 80
    Spain 80
    United Kingdom 80
  Latin America and Brazil
    United States 80
    Brazil 82
    Germany 82
    Netherlands 82
    United Kingdom 82
Bibliographies of Bibliographies
  General 82
  Latin America and Brazil 82

Luso-African and Other Lusophone Literatures

Bibliographies and Other Reference Works: Lusophone Africa 87
Bibliography: Portuguese in the United States 88

Index of Authors, Editors, and Compilers 91

Introduction

The present work is a classified, annotated, and selective guide to reference works that relate to the study of the Portuguese language or to Portuguese, Brazilian, or other Lusophone literatures. It originated as part of an intended larger bibliographical survey of Hispanic and Luso-Brazilian reference works that I undertook several years ago in cooperation with Hensley C. Woodbridge and José L. Freire. In it, I have followed many of the criteria for inclusion and organization that Woodbridge used in his 1983 work *Spanish and Spanish-American Literature: An Annotated Guide to Selected Bibliographies* (New York: MLA) and in his 1987 *Guide to Reference Works for the Study of the Spanish Language and Literature and Spanish American Literature* (New York: MLA), adding to them and attempting to adapt them to the Luso-Brazilian field.

For the purposes of this guide, the term "reference works" should be understood to include the following:

1. Bibliographies of the Portuguese language in the form of books or articles
2. Dictionaries of Portuguese of interest to language and literature students. (I include, for example, historical and etymological dictionaries and dictionaries of argot and popular speech but do not list dictionaries of technical, scientific, or commercial terms.)
3. Bibliographies of Portuguese, Brazilian, or other Lusophone literatures (or bibliographies that include listings of one or more of such literatures)
4. Dictionaries of literary terms related to Luso-Brazilian literature
5. Dictionaries of Portuguese or Brazilian authors and literature (or dictionaries that cover such authors or literature)
6. Bibliographies and dictionaries pertaining to specific Portuguese or Brazilian literary periods, genres, and regions
7. Book-length bibliographies and dictionaries pertaining to individual Portuguese or Brazilian authors. (Because of the dearth of such studies, I have made a few exceptions, including some shorter bibliographies but excluding many others, even though this meant leaving out certain authors. For a more complete listing of author bibliographies, consult David S. Zubatsky's works listed in items 284, 528, and 529.)
8. Bibliographies and lists of dissertations pertaining to Luso-Brazilian language and literature

9. Union lists and library and collection catalogs dealing with Portuguese or Brazilian literature
10. Library and resource guides covering Portuguese language and Portuguese, Brazilian, or Lusophone African literature
11. Bibliographies of translations, comparative studies, and cross-cultural scholarship related to Portuguese or Brazilian literature
12. Current bibliographies and periodical indexes in Portuguese language or Luso-Brazilian literature
13. Encyclopedias published in Portuguese. (These, for lack of a better place, were included in the language section.)
14. Book-length glossaries and vocabularies of Portuguese or Brazilian authors and works
15. Portuguese or Brazilian national bibliographies
16. Bibliographies of Portugal- or Brazil-related bibliographies and selected studies of some of the above-mentioned categories
17. Other, similar works

Not included, besides the aforementioned dictionaries of technical, scientific, and commercial terms, are such works as grammars, histories of literature, specialized literary or linguistic studies, orthographic dictionaries, and dictionaries of prepositions required by nouns, adjectives, or verbs.

The "Portuguese Language and Linguistics" section is designed more for the student of Luso-Brazilian language and literatures than it is for the student of linguistics. Works that relate to the Portuguese language and to one or both of the two major literatures often appear in the first, general category within the language section, although they may be listed in a more specialized category within the literature sections. Nevertheless, there are some categories listed in the literature sections (e.g., "Union Lists and Library and Collection Catalogs") whose items are not generally included in the language section, even though they may cover studies of the Portuguese language. Students will have to refer to the literature sections for information on such publications. Items in the "Portuguese Language and Linguistics" section are generally arranged alphabetically within a given category.

Listings are also normally alphabetical within categories in the section on Portuguese literature. There are, however, a few exceptions. Within the literary-period subcategories, general reference works usually appear first, followed by works on more specialized topics and, finally, by works dealing with individual authors, which are arranged chronologically by author's year of birth. Here, bibliographies are normally listed before dictionaries and glossaries. In addition, some categories, such as "Bibliographies of Translations" and "Comparative Literature and Cross-Cultural

Scholarship," are further divided into general studies and studies dealing with Portugal. For dissertations, works listing United States and Canadian dissertations are given first, moving from the general to the specific. These are followed by European, French, German and Austrian, and British and Irish listings, in that order. Similarly, the category dealing with union lists and library and collection catalogs, which is subdivided into "General" and "Portugal," begins with American and Canadian listings and continues with those of France, Spain, and the United Kingdom. In the section pertaining specifically to Portugal, listings of general catalogs, particularly in the United States, precede those of individual libraries.

The "Brazilian Literature" section, the most extensive of the bibliography, generally follows the organization of the "Portuguese Literature" section. It does, however, include a few subcategories not found in the preceding section. Moreover, in the "Latin America and Brazil" part of its "Bibliography of Bibliographies" category, I list together the Gropp bibliographies and their continuations even though this interrupts the otherwise alphabetical arrangement of the items.

The last section, "Luso-African and Other Lusophone Literatures," is the least extensive, owing to a general scarcity of reference works in this area. It is organized alphabetically by authors' surnames.

Most works listed herein were published since 1945. I have personally inspected the great majority of entries, having used the libraries of the University of California, Los Angeles; the University of California, Berkeley; the University of Southern California; the University of California, Irvine; California State University, Fullerton; and the University of Pittsburgh. Some works overlap several categories within a given section; I have usually chosen to list such works in what I considered the major category and have avoided cross-references. Thus, several items listed in the "Current Bibliographies and Periodical Indexes" category, for instance, could have been included too in the category on comparative literature and cross-cultural scholarship, but for the sake of brevity they have not been. For works that pertain to both Portuguese language and Portuguese, Brazilian, or Lusophone African literature or that pertain to two or more of the literatures, however, I have normally made the first mention the main listing and inserted cross-references in other sections where appropriate.

I have included, insofar as possible, annotations that reflect the contents of each item. In some entries, I have quoted from a work's introduction; in others—the majority—I have summarized the material or provided an abbreviated version of the table of contents. Annotations are, in general, more descriptive than critical. Several works have been singled out for their excellence or comprehensiveness.

It is hoped that the present work will serve as a guide for students, professors, and librarians interested in the language and literatures of the Luso-Brazilian world.

Bobby J. Chamberlain
University of Pittsburgh
4 February 1988

Portuguese Language and Linguistics

Bibliographies, Indexes, Catalogs, Guides, Directories, and Manuals of Works on the Portuguese of Portugal and Brazil

1. Almeida, Horácio de. *Catálogo de dicionários portugueses e brasileiros.* Rio de Janeiro: [Companhia Brasileira de Artes Gráficas], 1983. 132 pp. Lists alphabetically by author over 1,000 dictionaries, on a wide variety of topics, published in Brazil and Portugal. Not annotated.

2. Bach, Kathryn F., and Glanville Price. *Romance Linguistics and the Romance Languages: A Bibliography of Bibliographies.* Research Bibliographies and Checklists 22. London: Grant, 1977. 194 pp. A classified, annotated bibliography. Items 217–40 (99–105) and 243–46 (106–07) pertain to Portuguese.

3. "Bibliografía." *Revista de filología hispánica* 1–8 (1936–46); cont. in *Nueva revista de filología hispánica* 1– (1947–). Most issues include a classified listing of current materials in Portuguese language and literature. Reviews are cited. Authors are arranged chronologically within genres.

4. *Bibliografia dialectal galego-portuguesa.* Lisboa: Centro de Linguística, U de Lisboa, 1976. xxvii + 161 pp.

5. Câmara, Joaquim Mattoso, Jr. "Brazilian Linguistics." *Ibero-American and Caribbean Linguistics.* Ed. Thomas A. Sebeok et al. The Hague: Mouton, 1968. 229–47. Vol. 4 of *Current Trends in Linguistics.* Ed. Thomas A. Sebeok. 14 vols. 1963–76. A bibliographical essay, divided as follows: "Background," "General Linguistics," "Descriptive Linguistics," "Romance Linguistics," "Historical Study of Portuguese," "Dialectology," "Philology," "Stylistics," "Verse Technique," "Classical Philology," "Lexicography," "Final Remarks."

6. Comité International Permanent des Linguistes. *Bibliographie linguistique des années, 1939–1947.* 2 vols. Utrecht: Spectrum, 1949–50.

7.   ———. *Bibliographie linguistique de l'année.* Annual vols. for 1948-75. Utrecht: Spectrum, 1951-78.

8.   ———. *Bibliographie linguistique de l'année.* Annual vols. for 1976- . The Hague: Nijhoff, 1980- .
Perhaps the most comprehensive bibliography of linguistics. Lists books, articles, reviews, and dissertations. Classified.

9.   *Comparative Romance Language Newsletter.* 1- (1950-).
This bibliography, printed annually in the newsletter of the MLA's Comparative Romance Linguistics Discussion Group, includes a section on Portuguese language.

10.   Deal, Carl W. *Latin America and the Caribbean: A Dissertation Bibliography.* [Ann Arbor]: UMI, [1977]. 164 pp.
Catalogs all US PhD dissertations pertaining to Latin America published by University Microfilms International through the end of 1977. Arranged by disciplines, among which are "Language and Linguistics" (classified by language) and "Literature" (organized by country). Two supplements have been published: *Latin America and the Caribbean I: A Dissertation Bibliography,* for 1978-79, and *Latin America: A Catalog of Current Doctoral Dissertation Research,* for 1980-83.

11.   de Gorog, Ralph Paul. "Bibliografia de estudos do vocabulário português (1950-1965)." *Luso-Brazilian Review* 4.1 (1967): 83-110; 4.2 (1967): 95-110.
Lists Portuguese vocabulary studies published between 1950 and 1965. Contents: "Estudos etimológicos," "Estudos lexicais e semânticos," "Coisas e palavras," "O elemento estrangeiro no vocabulário de línguas estrangeiras," "Aditamentos às outras seções."

12.   Dietrich, Wolf. *Bibliografia da língua portuguesa do Brasil.* Tübingen: Narr, 1980. xxxii + 292 pp.
Contents: "Bibliografias e relatórios sobre investigação," "Anais, Atas de congressos, etc.," "Miscelâneas; Lingüística e filologia brasileira no Brasil e no estrangeiro," "O problema da diferenciação brasileira," "Norma lingüística no Brasil," "Níveis lingüísticos / A língua dos grupos sociais," "Geografia lingüística e dialetologia geral," "Descrição das zonas dialetais," "Influências estrangeiras no português do Brasil," "Ortografia," "Gramáticas, manuais, ensino do português no Brasil," "Fonética e fonologia," "Pronúncia, ortoepia, entoação," "Categorias gramaticais," "Morfologia," "Formação de palavras," "Sintaxe," "Semântica," "Vocabulários brasileiros anteriores a 1930 em ordem cronológica," "Léxico," "Línguas especiais: Gíria," "Terminologias," "Nomenclatura gramatical," "Toponímia e antroponímia," "Fraseologia—Locuções," "Etimologia e história das palavras," "Estudos diacrônicos (história da língua e gramática histórica)," "Categorias de textos, língua literária," "Estilística," "Autores," "Aquisição da linguagem, ensino," "Folclore e literatura popular." "Índice onomástico dos autores."
Very comprehensive. An extremely useful reference tool.

13.   Fernández, Oscar. *A Preliminary Listing of Foreign Periodical Holdings in the United States and Canada Which Give Coverage to Portuguese and Brazilian Language and Literature*. Iowa City: U of Iowa, 1968. vii + 28 pp.

Lists foreign journals and newspapers in US and Canadian libraries that deal with Luso-Brazilian language and literature.

14.   Geohegan, Abel Rodolfo. *Obras de referencia de América Latina: Repertorio selectivo y anotado de enciclopedias, diccionarios, bibliografías, repertorios biográficos, catálogos, guías, anuarios, índices, etc.* [Buenos Aires: Crisol, 1965]. 280 pp.

"Obra publicada con la ayuda de UNESCO."

A selective, classified, and annotated bibliography of the major "obras de referencia (enciclopedias, diccionarios, bibliografías, repertorios biográficos, catálogos, atlas, guías, anuarios, índices, etc., etc.) que se refieren a América Latina, sin importar el lugar de publicación o la materia del contenido." Includes sections on literature (207–14) and philology and linguistics (137–64). Lists titles in Portuguese as well as Spanish.

15.   Gillett, Theresa, and Helen McIntyre. *Catalog of Luso-Brazilian Material in the University of New Mexico Libraries*. Metuchen: Scarecrow, 1970. xiv + 961 pp.

Includes a section on Portuguese language (23–61) and an extensive section on Luso-Brazilian literature (62–385).

16.   Golden, Herbert H., and Seymour O. Simches. *Modern Iberian Language and Literature: A Bibliography of Homage Studies*. Cambridge: Harvard UP, 1958. x + 184 pp.

Includes linguistic studies of Portuguese and Brazilian Portuguese as well as works dealing with Portuguese literature, folklore, and culture. Lists 2,045 items.

17.   Harmon, Ronald M., and Bobby J. Chamberlain. *Brazil: A Working Bibliography in Literature, Linguistics, Humanities and the Social Sciences*. Special Study 14. Tempe: Arizona State U, Center for Latin American Studies, 1975. viii + 101 pp.

Contents: "Bibliographies and Biobibliographies on Various Aspects of Brazilian Studies," "General Literary Histories," "Literary Periods," "Literary Genres," "Special Topics in Literature," "Literary Criticism," "Dictionaries of Literature," "Literary Anthologies," "Journals, Magazines, and Supplements Important to Literature," "Linguistics and Philology," "General Background on Brazil," "Geography," "History and Politics," "Economics," "Culture and Civilization," "Sociology, Ethnology, and Anthropology," "Philosophy," "Art, Architecture, and Cinematography," "Music," "Religion," "Folklore."

Lists major reference works and basic source materials for the study of the areas indicated. There is a heavy emphasis on literature; approximately half of the bibliography is devoted to literary topics. Not annotated. Author index.

18.   Hoge, Henry W. *A Selective Bibliography of Luso-Brazilian Linguistics*. Milwaukee: U of Wisconsin Language and Area Center for Latin America, 1966.

An unannotated bibliography listing over 900 works that deal for the most part with Brazilian Portuguese. A revised edition (Rio de Janeiro, 1968, 85 pp.) was also published.

19.   Jackson, William Vernon. *Library Guide for Brazilian Studies*. Pittsburgh: U of Pittsburgh Book Centers, 1964. xiii + 197 pp.
A guide to the use of the Brazilian holdings of US university libraries. Includes a section on language and literature (31-40).

20.   Manuppella, Giacinto. *Os estudos de filologia portuguesa de 1930 a 1949: Subsídios bibliográficos*. Lisboa: Inst. para a Alta Cultura, 1950. 246 pp.
A classified bibliography. Lists philological studies published in Portugal and Brazil during the period indicated. Includes an author index.

21.   Modern Language Association of America. *MLA Directory of Periodicals: A Guide to Journals and Series in Languages and Literature*. New York: MLA, 1979- .
Provides information on over 3,000 periodicals relating to languages and literatures. Entries are arranged alphabetically by title. Detailed subject, sponsoring organization, editor, and language indexes. Updated biennially.

22.   ———. *MLA International Bibliography of Books and Articles on the Modern Languages and Literatures*. New York: MLA, 1956- .
Before 1956 listed only works published in the United States. Currently, volume 3 is devoted to linguistics; Portuguese, Brazilian, and Lusophone African literatures are included in volume 2. Literary studies are organized within a given language by period and writer. Includes author and subject indexes.

23.   Moraes, Rubens Borba de, and William Berrien. *Manual bibliográfico de estudos brasileiros*. Rio de Janeiro: Souza, 1949. xi + 895 pp.
Long a standard reference work in these fields. Includes sections on philology (257-84) and literature (classified; 639-739). Each section or subsection contains an introduction written by its compiler.

24.   Musso Ambrosi, Luis Alberto. *Bibliografía uruguaya sobre Brasil: Libros y folletos referentes al Brasil o de autores brasileños, impresos en el Uruguay*. 2nd ed., enl. Montevideo: Inst. de Cultura Uruguayo-Brasileño, 1973. 166 pp.
First edition, 1967. A classified bibliography. Sections include "Literatura" (93-103) and "Lenguaje" (79-83). Onomastic index.

25.   Naro, Anthony M. "Portuguese in Brazil." *Language and Philology in Romance*. Ed. Rebecca Posner and John N. Green. Vol. 3 of *Trends in Romance Linguistics and Philology*. Trends in Linguistics. Studies and Monographs 14. The Hague: Mouton, 1982. 413-62.
A bibliographical essay divided as follows: "1. Introduction," "2. Philology," "2.1. Sousa da Silveira to Celso Cunha," "2.2. Critical Editions," "2.3. Dialectology," "2.4. Philological Grammar," "2.5. Philological Periodicals and Congress Proceedings," "3. Linguistics," "3.1. Mattoso Câmara," "3.2. Synchronic

and Diachronic Linguistics," "3.3. Journals," "4. Conclusions and Perspectives for the Future."

26.   "Notas bibliográficas. . . ." *Revista portuguesa de filologia.* Coimbra. 1947– .
An annual classified bibliography prepared by M. Paiva Boléo. Lists Luso-Brazilian linguistic and literary studies.

27.   Pereira, Benjamim Enes. *Bibliografia analítica de etnografia portuguesa.* Lisboa: Inst. de Alta Cultura, 1965. xv + 672 pp.
An annotated, classified bibliography. Lists studies of popular vocabulary and language and of popular theater.

28.   Porter, Dorothy B. *Afro-Braziliana: A Working Bibliography.* Boston: Hall, 1978. xxii + 294 pp.
A classified bibliography. Lists works on Africanisms in Brazilian Portuguese. There is a section on literature (135–70). Also lists works by many Brazilian authors who deal with Afro-Brazilian topics, as well as critical and biographical studies pertaining to such works and authors.

29.   Primus, Wilma J. *Creole and Pidgin Languages in the Caribbean: A Select Bibliography.* St. Augustine, Trinidad: Library of the U of the West Indies, n.d. iii + 80 pp.
Includes works on "Spanish/Portuguese based creoles and pidgins" (68–74).

30.   Reinecke, John E., et al. *A Bibliography of Pidgin and Creole Languages.* Oceanic Linguistics Special Publications 14. Honolulu: UP of Hawaii, 1975.
An annotated bibliography written by a team of scholars. Includes a section on Brazilian Portuguese and the question of creolization and *língua geral.*

31.   Rogers, Francis M., and David T. Haberly. *Brazil, Portugal and Other Portuguese-Speaking Lands: A List of Books Primarily in English.* Cambridge: Harvard UP, 1968. 73 pp.
A classified bibliography of books, published in English and other languages (with the exception of Portuguese), on various aspects of Brazil, Portugal, and other Portuguese-speaking areas. Includes sections on Portuguese language (8–9), the Portuguese of Brazil (67–69), Portuguese literature (40–47), and Brazilian literature (69–72). Not annotated.

32.   Rohlfs, Gerhard. *Manual de filología hispánica: Guía bibliográfica, crítica y metódica.* Trans. Carlos Patiño Rosselli. Publicaciones del Instituto Caro y Cuervo 12. Bogotá: Inst. Caro y Cuervo, 1957. 377 pp.
Classified and annotated. Listings pertaining to Portuguese philology are on 275–347. Author, subject, word, and onomastic indexes.

33.   *Romanische Bibliographie.* Tübingen: Niemeyer, 1967– .
Previously published as an annual supplement to *Zeitschrift für romanische Philologie* 1875–76–79– ; volumes cover 1940–50, 1951–55, 1956–60, 1961–62,

and 1963–64 but not 1914–23. Includes classified sections devoted to Portuguese linguistics and Luso-Brazilian literatures. Lists reviews. One of the most thorough bibliographies published.

34.   Schmidt-Radefeldt, Jürgen. "Modern Portuguese Linguistics: A Selective Bibliography of the Synchronic Description of Portuguese and Brazilian Portuguese." *Readings in Portuguese Linguistics.* Ed. Jürgen Schmidt-Radefeldt. Amsterdam: North-Holland, 1976. 447–73.
Contents: "Grammars and Grammatical Aspects," "Phonetics and Phonology," "Morphology and Syntax," "Semantics and Lexicon," "Teaching Portuguese." Lists 230 items.

35.   Sletsjøe, Leif. "Les études portugaises dans les pays scandinaves." *Actes du quatrième Congrès des Romanistes Scandinaves publiés à l'occasion du soixantième anniversaire de Holger Sten.* Copenhague: Akademisk, 1967. 163–79.
A bibliographical essay on the studies of Portuguese written by Scandinavians.

36.   Sodré, Nelson Werneck. *O que se deve ler para conhecer o Brasil.* 5th ed. Rio de Janeiro: Civilização Brasileira, 1976. 377 pp.
Includes sections that list and comment on what the author regards as essential and subsidiary sources for the study of Brazilian Portuguese (266–70) and Brazilian literature (306–15). First edition, 1945.

37.   Valis, Noël. "Directory of Publication Sources in the Fields of Hispanic Language and Literature." *Hispania* 64 (1981): 226–57.
Intended as a publishing guide for Hispanists. Supplies information on 265 Hispanic and Luso-Brazilian journals, to which the author submitted questionnaires.

38.   Williams, Harry Franklin. *An Index of Medieval Studies Published in Festschriften, 1865–1946, with Special Reference to Romanic Material.* Berkeley: U of California P, 1951. 165 pp.
Lists 5,238 studies published in 490 volumes.

39.   *The Year's Work in Modern Language Studies.* Cambridge: Modern Humanities Research Assn.
Annual volumes cover 1931–39 and 1950–   ; volume 11 covers 1940–49. Includes sections on Portuguese language, Portuguese literature, and Brazilian literature. Sections are arranged by subject and chronological period. Each volume has an index of critics and subjects. Each section carries the name of its compiler. Brief critical comments are included.

40.   Zubatsky, David S. "A Bibliography of Cumulative Indexes to Luso-Brazilian Journals of the Nineteenth and Twentieth Centuries: Humanities and Social Sciences." *Luso-Brazilian Review* 8.2 (1971): 71–81.
An annotated bibliography of the cumulative indexes of 88 nineteenth- and twentieth-century Luso-Brazilian journals devoted to humanities and the social sciences.

41. ———. "An Index to Galician and Portuguese (including Brazilian) Linguistic Studies in Festschriften." *Luso-Brazilian Review* 11.2 (1974): 237–53; 12.1 (1975): 3–33.
Lists linguistic articles appearing in festschriften or homage volumes published between 1884 and 1972. Includes 473 titles.

42. ———. "An International Bibliography of Cumulative Indexes to Journals Publishing Articles on Hispanic Languages and Literatures." *Hispania* 58 (1975): 76–107.
"Arrangement is by country and then alphabetical by journal title. Items included in each annotation, when available and applicable, are found in the following order: (1) original place of publication; (2) date the review began, and, if defunct, the date it ceased publication; (3) publishing organization; (4) index(es) of its contents; and, finally, (5) the type of index(es)" (76). Includes cumulative indexes of both Portuguese and Brazilian journals.

43. ———. "An International Bibliography of Cumulative Indices to Journals Publishing Articles on Hispanic Languages and Literatures: First Supplement." *Hispania* 67 (1984): 383–93.
Supplement to no. 42.

Etymological Dictionaries

44. Bueno, Francisco da Silveira. *Grande dicionário etimológico-prosódico da língua portuguesa.* 8 vols. São Paulo: Saraiva, 1963–67.
Vol. 1 (A): xxxiii + 462 pp.; vol. 2 (B–D): 463–1054; vol. 3 (E–F): 1055–498; vol. 4 (G–K): 1497–2059; vol. 5 (L–M): 2061–568; vol. 6 (N–P): 2569–3270; vol. 7 (Q–S): 3271–865; vol. 8 (T–Z): 3867–4338
"O nosso dicionário intitula-se, prevalentemente *etimológico*, mas é também *prosódico*. Dá, em primeiro lugar, a etimologia da palavra; depois o significado, a pronúncia dos casos duvidosos, acrescentando ainda *sinônimos*. Na parte da etimologia, quando há controvérsias, damos as opiniões mais importantes, determinando-nos por uma delas que nos pareça mais fundamentada. Muitas vezes, não admitimos nenhuma delas, oferecendo a nossa explicação" (xxiv). The author goes on to criticize the procedure of Antenor Nascentes and others who, he says, present the opinions of several etymologists without passing judgment on any of them.

45. Cunha, Antônio Geraldo da. *Dicionário etimológico Nova Fronteira da língua portuguesa.* Rio de Janeiro: Nova Fronteira, 1982. xxix + 839 pp.
"Assistentes: Cláudio Mello Sobrinho, Diva de Oliveira Salles, Gilda da Costa Pinto, Júlio César Castañon Guimarães, Suelí Guimarães Gomes."
A handy, single-volume reference tool, designed especially for students and professors of language and literature, as well as for linguists, scientists, professionals, and other scholars. Bibliography.

46. Machado, José Pedro. *Dicionário etimológico da língua portuguesa: Com a mais antiga documentação escrita e conhecida de muitos dos vocábulos estudados.* 2nd ed. 5 vols. Lisboa: Confluência, 1967. Vol. 1 (A–B): 478 pp.; vol. 2 (C–E): 521 pp.; vol. 3 (F–L): 454 pp.; vol. 4 (M–P): 465 pp.; vol. 5 (Q–Z): 439 pp.

A classic study; the most authoritative etymological dictionary of the Portuguese language. First edition, 1952. There is also a third edition (Lisboa: Horizonte, 1977).

47. Lorenzo, Ramón. *Sobre cronologia do vocabulário galego-português: Anotações ao Dicionário etimológico de José Pedro Machado.* Vigo: Galaxia, 1968. xii + 382 pp.

It is, according to the author, "uma melhoria de muitas datas apresentadas por Machado no seu Dicionário, acrescentado de muitas palavras não importadas no mesmo."

48. Nascentes, Antenor. *Dicionário etimológico da língua portuguesa.* Vol. 1. Rio de Janeiro: Alves, 1932. Vol. 2, *Nomes próprios.* Rio de Janeiro: Académica; São José; Alves; Livros de Portugal, 1952. xxvii + 389 pp.

A classic study. Volume 1 includes common nouns, and volume 2 examines proper nouns. Volume 1 was reprinted in 1955.

49. ———. *Dicionário etimológico resumido.* Rio de Janeiro: Inst. Nacional do Livro, Ministério da Educação e Cultura, 1966. 791 pp.

Following the example of Joan Corominas, Nascentes created this abbreviated version of his *Dicionário etimológico da língua portuguesa* (no. 48). Includes a brief bibliography.

Historical Dictionaries

50. Cunha, Antônio Geraldo da. *Dicionário histórico das palavras de origem tupi.* São Paulo: Melhoramentos; Brasília: Inst. Nacional do Livro, 1978. 357 pp.

Provides detailed etymologies and extensive documentation and historical quotations for each item. Includes a comprehensive bibliography.

51. Messner, Dieter. *Dictionnaire chronologique des langues ibéroromanes. I. Dictionnaire chronologique portugais.* Heidelberg: Carl Winter Universitätsverlag, 1976. xi + 488 pp.

A comparative chronological dictionary of Portuguese, Spanish, Catalan, and French vocabularies from the tenth century to 1949. Organized from the standpoint of Portuguese chronology. Lists approximately 29,000 modern Portuguese lexical items.

52. Magne, Augusto. *Dicionário da língua portuguesa (especialmente dos períodos medieval e clássico).* 2 vols. Rio de Janeiro: Ministério da Edu-

cação e Saúde, Inst. Nacional do Livro, 1950–54.
Vol. 1 (A–Af): lxxvi + 578 pp.; vol. 2 (Ag–Al): xvi + 238 pp.
Magne died in 1966.

53.   Viterbo, Frei Joaquim de Santa Rosa de. *Elucidário das palavras, termos e frases que em Portugal antigamente se usavam e que hoje regularmente se ignoram: Obra indispensável para entender sem erro os documentos mais raros e preciosos que entre nós se conservam.* Edição crítica . . . por Mário Fiúza. 2 vols. Porto: Civilização, 1965.
Vol. 1 (A): 738 + 60 pp.; vol. 2 (B–Z): 779 pp.
First edition, 1798–99. A historical dictionary of medieval Portuguese terms. Uses quotations from texts.

54.   Dalgado, Sebastião Rodolfo. *Glossário luso-asiático.* 2 vols. Hamburg: Buske, 1982.
Vol. 1 (A–L): 12 + lxvii + 535 pp.; vol. 2 (M–Z): x + 580 pp.
A reprint of the original Coimbra edition (1919, 1921). With an introduction in German by Joseph M. Piel. Contains an introductory study and an extensive bibliography. Lists, defines, and gives the etymology of Asiatic terms that were incorporated into Portuguese during the period of explorations and the colonial era and that appear in Portuguese literature of the Orient.

Dictionaries of Modern Portuguese

55.   Academia Brasileira de Letras. *Dicionário da língua portuguesa.* Elaborado por Antenor Nascentes. 4 vols. Rio de Janeiro: Nacional, 1961–67.
Vol. 1 (A–C): xv + 587 pp.; vol. 2 (D–I): 599 pp.; vol. 3 (J–P): 479 pp.; vol. 4 (Q–Z): 436 pp.
An official, long-standing project of the Brazilian Academy of Letters; the first of its kind in Brazil.

56.   Academia das Ciências de Lisboa. *Dicionário da língua portuguesa.* Lisboa: Nacional; Moeda, 1976–   .
Vol. 1 (A–Azuverte): cxv + 678 pp.
A project of the Academy. Since the lexicon was initiated before 1971, the orthography is not completely modernized.

57.   Aulete, Francisco Júlio Caldas. *Dicionário contemporâneo da língua portuguesa em 5 volumes.* 2nd Brazilian ed., rev. and enl. 5 vols. Rio de Janeiro: Delta, 1964.
A standard reference work. The first Brazilian edition (the fourth edition overall) was published in 1958, updated, revised, and enlarged, with Brazilian terms, by Hamílcar Garcia. The third Brazilian edition was published in 5 volumes (Lisboa: Delta, 1980).

58.   Carvalho, J., and Vicente Peixoto. *Dicionário da língua portuguesa.* 19th ed., rev. and enl. São Paulo: Lep, 1971. 1,066 pp.
"Revisto e ampliado por F. J. da Silva Ramos, ilustrado por Jean Carlo Ruben Azevedo. . . ."
"[I]nteiramente revista e remodelada de acordo com a nomenclatura gramatical brasileira por Ubiratan Rosa."

59.   *Dicionário Melhoramentos da língua portuguesa.* São Paulo: Melhoramentos, 1977. 1,035 pp.
A handy reference volume designed mainly for students. The orthography conforms to that of the 1971 law.

60.   *Dicionário moderno da língua portuguesa.* Comp. Afonso Telles Alves. Rev. ed. 3 vols. São Paulo: EDIGRAF, 1961.
Vol. 1 (A–D): 341 pp.; vol. 2 (E–N): 347–694; vol. 3 (O–Z): 699–1108.
Contains an appendix with an explanation of the official Brazilian orthography of the period. According to Alves, the work is directed not at the specialist but at the general public.

61.   *Dicionário prático ilustrado.* Porto: Lello, 1960. 1,966 pp.
"Novo dicionário enciclopédico luso-brasileiro publicado sob a direcção de Jaime de Séguier. Edição actualizada e aumentada por José Lello e Edgar Lello."
"Edição feita de acordo com a Livraria Larousse, de Paris."
Contains, besides the dictionary illustrated with photos, pictures, tables, and maps, an encyclopedic section (also illustrated), a compendium of Portuguese grammar, a glossary of foreign and Latin terms and expressions, and tables of universal history, mathematical symbols, and the metric system. Recalls the *Petit Larousse.*

62.   Fernandes, Francisco, with the collaboration of F. Marques Guimarães. *Dicionário da língua portuguesa.* 2 vols. Rio de Janeiro: Globo, 1958.
Vol. 1 (A–H): 1,091 pp.; vol. 2 (I–Z): 1093–2217.
An expanded version of the *Dicionário brasileiro contemporâneo.* Contains appendixes with "palavras e locuções latinas e estrangeiras," "nomes próprios locativos, personativos e mitológicos," a "ligeiro estudo sobre verbos portugueses," and notes on orthography.

63.   Fernandes, Francisco, and F. Marques Guimarães. *Dicionário brasileiro contemporâneo.* 4th ed., rev. and enl. Porto Alegre: Globo, 1975. 1,392 pp.
First edition, 1953. According to the authors, "nosso objetivo principal foi condensar, num volume de formato cômodo e popular, aquilo que um dicionário de porte médio deve conter, todas as informações que possam interessar aos leitores a quem se destina, particularmente aos estudantes do curso secundário e aos homens de trabalho. . . ." Orthography conforms to that of the 1971 law.

64.   Ferreira, Aurélio Buarque de Holanda. *Novo dicionário da língua portuguesa.* 2nd ed., rev. and enl. Rio de Janeiro: Nova Fronteira, 1986. xxiii + 1,838 pp.
"Assistentes: Margarida dos Anjos, Marina Baird Ferreira, Elza Tavares Fer-

reira, Joaquim Campelo Marques, Stella Rodrigo Octávio Moutinho; auxiliar: Giovani Mafra e Silva."
First edition, 1975. The second edition has been enlarged by a third. Perhaps the best dictionary of the Portuguese language available in a single volume. Contains more than 100,000 entries and subentries, including a great wealth of neologisms and slang terms and expressions. Represents a monumental expansion and updating of the materials included in the *Pequeno dicionário brasileiro da língua portuguesa* (no. 65), also compiled by Ferreira. A fundamental reference work. On the cover: "Novo dicionário Aurélio da língua portuguesa."

65.   Ferreira, Aurélio Buarque de Holanda, with the assistance of João Baptista da Luz. *Pequeno dicionário brasileiro da língua portuguesa.* 11th ed. Rio de Janeiro: Civilização Brasileira, 1968. xxxiii + 1,301 pp.
For many years the most popular single-volume dictionary of Brazilian Portuguese. The eleventh edition has been enlarged by a fourth. Also contains orthographical instructions (1943) and a list of foreign words and expressions used in Portuguese.

66.   Freire, Laudelino, and J. L. de Campos. *Grande e novíssimo dicionário da língua portuguesa.* 2nd ed. 5 vols. Rio de Janeiro: Olympio, 1954.
Vol. 1 (A–Az): xxx + 928 pp.; vol. 2 (B–D): x + 930–2017; vol. 3 (E–I): x + 2019–3052; vol. 4 (J–P): x + 3053–4209; vol. 5 (Q–Z): x + 4211–5363.
A notable reference work. Third edition, 1957.

67.   Gueriós, Rosário Farani Mansur. *Dicionário cultural da língua portuguesa.* 4 vols. Curitiba: GRAFIPAR, 1967.
Vol. 1 (A–C): 413 pp.; vol. 2 (D–H): 366 pp.; vol. 3 (I–O): 244 pp.; vol. 4 (P–Z): 450 pp.

68.   Houaiss, Antônio. *Pequeno dicionário enciclopédico Koogan Larousse.* Rio de Janeiro: Larousse do Brasil, 1979. xx + 1,644 pp.
Follows the format of the *Petit Larousse*, using many of the same materials, in addition to many new materials related specifically to Brazil. The first part is a dictionary, and the second is an encyclopedia. Contains numerous illustrations, tables, and maps. Extremely useful.

69.   Magalhães, Álvaro, et al. *Dicionário enciclopédico brasileiro ilustrado.* 2 vols. Rio de Janeiro: Globo, [1960].
Vol. 1 (A–F): xxxii + 1,178 pp.; vol. 2 (G–Z): viii + 1179–2627.
First edition, 1943. Contains many photographs, drawings, maps, and color plates, in addition to definitions of selected terms and brief articles on chosen topics.

70.   *Novo dicionário brasileiro Melhoramentos ilustrado.* 6th ed., rev. 5 vols. São Paulo: Melhoramentos, 1970.
Vol. 1 (A–B): 678 pp.; vol. 2 (C–E): 936 pp.; vol. 3 (F–M): 863 pp.; vol. 4 (N–R): 751 pp.; vol. 5 (S–Z): 724 pp.
The first edition, *Novo dicionário brasileiro*, was published in 4 volumes in 1962–63, under the direction of Adalberto Prado e Silva. There is also a

more recent version: *Grande dicionário brasileiro Melhoramentos ilustrado* (1975).

71.   Quadros, Jânio, with the collaboration of Ubiratan Rosa. *Novo dicionário prático da língua portuguesa*. São Paulo: Rideel, 1976. 1,213 pp.
"Não fizemos obra para doutos, ou que por doutos se inculcam, nem para lexicógrafos ou estilistas, mas para os estudantes e o povo, na sua generalidade" (12). The author is a former president of Brazil.

72.   Silva, António de Morais. *Grande dicionário da língua portuguesa*. 10th ed., rev. and enl. by Augusto Moreno, Cardoso Júnior, and José Pedro Machado. 12 vols. Lisboa: Confluência, 1948–60.
Vol. 1 (A–Ar): 1,115 pp.; vol. 2 (Ar–Ces): 1,115 pp.; vol. 3 (Ces–Des): 1,115 pp.; vol. 4 (Des–Eza): 1,052 pp.; vol. 5 (F–Iri): 1,046 pp.; vol. 6 (Iri–Mor): 956 pp.; vol. 7 (Mor–Pea): 956 pp.; vol. 8 (Peç–Pv): 898 pp.; vol. 9 (Q–Sei): 1,004 pp.; vol. 10 (Sei–Tom): 956 pp.; vol. 11 (Tom–Zuz): 906 pp.; vol. 12 (supp.; comp. José Pedro Machado): 1,099 pp.
A classic reference work. First edition, 1813. On the cover: "Dicionário de Morais. 10 edição."

73.   Soares, Antônio Joaquim de Macedo. *Dicionário brasileiro da língua portuguesa: Elucidário etimológico crítico das palavras e frases que, originárias do Brasil, ou que populares, se não encontram nos dicionários da língua portuguesa, ou neles vêm com forma ou significação diferente*. Ed. and completed by Julião Rangel de Macedo Soares. 2 vols. Rio de Janeiro: Inst. Nacional do Livro, 1954–55.
Vol. 1 (A–L): xxxi + 275 pp.; vol. 2 (M–Z): 207 pp.
The *Dicionário*'s first appearance in print was in 1888, when the *Anais da Biblioteca Nacional* published an excerpt that included up to the word *candieiro*. Includes many etymologies.

74.   Zúquete, Afonso. *Dicionário geral luso-brasileiro da língua portuguesa*. Lisboa: Enciclopédia, 1963– .
Vol. 1 (A–Apel): 1963, 957 pp.; vol. 2 (Apen–Cang): 1966, 957 pp.; vol. 3 (Cang–Damb): 736 pp.

Synonyms and Antonyms

75.   Azevedo, Francisco Ferreira dos Santos. *Dicionário analógico da língua portuguesa*. Brasília: Coordenadora-Thesaurus, 1983. 685 pp.
Arguably the best thesaurus of the Portuguese language.

76.   Costa, Agenor. *Dicionário de sinônimos e locuções da língua portuguesa*. 3rd ed. 5 vols. Rio de Janeiro: Fundo de Cultura, 1967.
Vol. 1 (A–B): 427 pp.; vol. 2 (C–D): 427–878; vol. 3 (E–I): 879–1377; vol. 4 (J–P): 1377–1900; vol. 5 (Q–Z): 1901–2370.

"Reunindo a sinonímia e as locuções de dezessete dicionários, com seus significados nas ordens direta e inversa." First edition, Rio de Janeiro: Nacional, 1950.

77. Fernandes, Francisco. *Dicionário de sinônimos e antônimos da língua portuguesa.* 3rd ed., rev. and enl. by Celso Pedro Luft. Porto Alegre: Globo, 1980. 870 pp.
First edition, 1945. For many years the best dictionary of Portuguese synonyms and antonyms available in Brazil.

78. Nascentes, Antenor. *Dicionário de sinônimos.* 3rd ed. Rio de Janeiro: Nova Fronteira, 1981. 487 pp.
A scholarly study; limited to synonyms. First edition, 1957. Second edition, "revista e aumentada" (Rio de Janeiro: Livros de Portugal, 1969). The third edition was overseen by Olavo Aníbal Nascentes. Contains an index.

Bilingual Dictionaries

79. Houaiss, Antônio. *Webster: Dicionário inglês-português.* Rio de Janeiro: Record, 1982. 928 pp.
Published as volume 1 of the Webster dictionary. Volume 2 is a reprint of the Taylor Portuguese-English lexicon (no. 82). Volume 1 contains more than 100,000 entries. The emphasis is on Brazilian Portuguese.

80. *The New Appleton Dictionary of the English and Portuguese Languages.* Ed. Antônio Houaiss and Catherine B. Avery. New York: Appleton, 1964. xx + 636 + xx + 665 pp.
Associate editor: José E. A. do Prado; assistant editors: Edna Jansen de Mello Clarke and Fernando Antônio de Mello Vianna.
Arguably the best single-volume Portuguese-English, English-Portuguese dictionary. In need of updating, it is, regrettably, out of print. The emphasis is on Brazilian Portuguese. Includes tables of weights and measures and lists of common abbreviations, foreign words commonly used in Portuguese, numbers, and Portuguese verb conjugations.

81. *Novo Michaelis dicionário ilustrado.* 2 vols. São Paulo: Melhoramentos, 1979.
Vol. 1 (Inglês-Português): 24th ed., xxxii + 1,123 pp.; vol. 2 (Português-Inglês): 22nd ed., li + 1,320 pp.
Fritz Pietzschke is indicated as the editor of volume 1. Both volumes are illustrated. Includes lists of verb conjugations, abbreviations, weights and measures, and the like. Considered to be one of the best bilingual dictionaries for Portuguese and English. Subsequent editions.

82. Taylor, James L. *A Portuguese-English Dictionary.* Revised ed. Stanford: Stanford UP, 1970. xx + 662 pp.

"With corrections and additions by the author and Priscilla Clark Martin." Defines some 60,000 Portuguese entries in English. The emphasis is on Brazilian Portuguese. Contains orthographic, pronunciation, and verb-conjugation charts. Highly regarded. Also reprinted as volume 2 of the Webster bilingual dictionary (Rio de Janeiro: Record, 1982). See no. 79.

Word Formation

83.   Olteanu, Tudora Sandru. "Bibliografía de los trabajos relativos a la formación de palabras en los idiomas iberorrománicos (1920–1970)." *Boletín de filología española* 42–45 (1972): 13–35.
Divided into 2 parts; the second part lists works dealing with word formation in Portuguese. Not annotated. Includes 281 entries.

Onomastics

84.   Boléo, Manuel Paiva. "Bibliographie onomastique de Portugal." *Onoma* 6 (1955–56): 1–15.
Divided into: "Generalia," "Toponymie," "Anthroponymie."
Continues in other years with several different compilers.

85.   Gueriós, Rosário Farani Mansur. *Dicionário etimológico de nomes e sobrenomes.* 2nd ed., rev. and enl. São Paulo: Ave Maria, 1973. 231 pp.
First edition, 1949. Introduction (15–43). Bibliography.

86.   Nascentes, Antenor. *Dicionário etimológico da língua portuguesa.* Vol. 2, *Nomes próprios.* See no. 48.

Encyclopedias

87.   *Grande enciclopédia Delta Larousse.* 15 vols. Rio de Janeiro: Delta, 1972.
Vol. 1 (A–Ara): 448 pp.; vol. 2 (Ara–Ble): 449–928; vol. 3 (Ble–Car): 929–1408; vol. 4 (Car–Cor): 1409–904; vol. 5 (Cor–Emb): 1905–2384; vol. 6 (Emb–Fra): 2385–864; vol. 7 (Fra–Het): 2865–3344; vol. 8 (Het–Kör): 3345–836; vol. 9 (Kör–Mar): 3837–4328; vol. 10 (Mar–Nor): 4329–840; vol. 11 (Nor–Pia): 4841–5316; vol. 12 (Pia–Rev): 5317–792; vol. 13 (Rev–Ser): 5793–6268; vol. 14 (Ser–Tra): 6269–728; vol. 15 (Tra–Zyr): 6729–7180.
"Editoria: Antônio Houaiss." A monumental reference work. Many color plates. A yearbook is also published.

88.   *Grande enciclopédia portuguesa e brasileira.* 42 vols. to date. Lisboa: Enciclopédia, 1935– . Vols. 1–40: 1935–60; 2nd pt. (Brasil), 2 vols. to date: 1967– .
Vol. 1 (A–Alma): 973 pp.; vol. 2 (Alma–Apua): 1,033 pp.; vol. 3 (Apua–Bail): 1,033 pp.; vol. 4 (Bail–Brag): 1,049 pp.; vol. 5 (Brag–Carr): 1,004 pp.; vol. 6 (Carr–Coca): 1,020 pp.; vol. 7 (Cocai–Creci): 1,020 pp.; vol. 8 (Crede–Dilar): 1,020 pp.; vol. 9 (Dilat–Escar): 1,020 pp.; vol. 10 (Escar–Febra): 1,017 pp.; vol. 11 (Febre–Gabao): 1,024 pp.; vol. 12 (Gabar–Heha): 1,017 pp.; vol. 13 (Heide–Irapu): 1,018 pp.; vol. 14 (Iraqu–Levan): 1, 018 pp.; vol. 15 (Levar–Maldi): 1,002 pp.; vol. 16 (Maldo–Mermi): 1,101 pp.; vol. 17 (Mermo–Moura): 1,003 pp.; vol. 18 (Moura–Nuck): 999 pp.; vol. 19 (Nucle–Paisd): 1,001 pp.; vol. 20 (Paise–Penim): 1,000 pp.; vol. 21 (Penin–Pisot): 999 pp.; vol. 22 (Pispe–Povol): 999 pp.; vol. 23 (Povor–Quere): 938 pp.; vol. 24 (Quere–Relat): 920 pp.; vol. 25 (Relat–Rodri): 938 pp.; vol. 26 (Rodri–Sanch): 921 pp.; vol. 27 (Sanch–Seare): 922 pp.; vol. 28 (Seba–Silve): 922 pp.; vol. 29 (Silve–Soute): 920 pp.; vol. 30 (Soute–Tedes): 921 pp.; vol. 31 (Tedeu–Tomar): 925 pp.; vol. 32 (Tomar–Trist): 921 pp.; vol. 33 (Trita–Vales): 922 pp.; vol. 34 (Valet–Viana): 919 pp.; vol. 35 (Viana–Vilar): 920 pp.; vol. 36 (Vilar–Worce): 920 pp.; vol. 37 (Words–Al [Apêndice]): 922 pp.; vol. 38 (Al–Be): 924 pp.; vol. 39 (Be–Li): 954 pp.; vol. 40 (Li–Zz): 853 + lxxvi pp. 2nd pt.: Brasil: vol. 1 (Aanga–Calad): 956 pp.; vol. 2 (Calaf–Geise): 940 pp.
The largest Portuguese-language encyclopedia. Illustrated. Volumes 37–40 are an appendix.

89.   Silveira, Alarico. *Enciclopédia brasileira.* Rio de Janeiro: Inst. Nacional do Livro, 1958– .
Vol. 1 (A–Anzol-de-tenda): 589 pp.
Sponsored by the Fundação Edmundo Bittencourt.

90.   Vieira [de Mello], Antenor. *Pequena enciclopédia da língua portuguesa.* 11 vols. Rio de Janeiro: Livros do Brasil, 1964–65.
Vol. 1, *Gramática expositiva sintética*: 312 pp.; vol. 2, *Verbos regulares*: 304 pp.; vol. 3, *Verbos irregulares*: 328 pp.; vol. 4, *Breviário de facilidades*: 318 pp.; vol. 5, *Dicionário de linguagem* ("Plural de compostos," "Coletivos e correlatos," "Erros e dúvidas," "Do latim ao português," "Provérbios e máximas"): 352 pp.; vol. 6, *Dicionário de oratória e literatura*: 332 pp.; vol. 7, *Dicionário de sinônimos, antônimos, parônimos, homônimos (A–G)*: 332 pp.; vol. 8, *Dicionário de sinônimos, antônimos, parônimos, homônimos (H–Z)*: 304 pp.; vol. 9, *Vocabulário geral (A–D)*; vol. 10, *Vocabulário geral (E–N)*; vol. 11, *Vocabulário geral (O–Z)*.

Dictionaries of Popular Expressions, Regionalisms, and Argot

Portugal

91.　Costa, Alexandre de Carvalho. *Nótulas etnográficas e linguísticas alentejanas apresentadas em expressões populares.* Portalegre: Junta Distrital de Portalegre, 1964. 293 pp.
Explains and discusses 140 Portuguese popular expressions from Alentejo.

92.　Delgado, Manuel Joaquim. *A linguagem popular do Baixo-Alentejo.* Beja: N.p., 1951. 218 pp.
Lists terms and regional variants from Baixo-Alentejo. Often cites popular verses that include such lexical items.

93.　Dias, Jaime Lopes. *A linguagem popular da Beira Baixa: Apontamentos.* Lisboa: Revista de História e Cultura, 1962. 113 pp.
Records Portuguese regionalisms of Beira Baixa. Includes an appendix with recent additions to the vocabulary.

94.　Lapa, Albino. *Dicionário de calão.* 2nd ed. Lisboa: Presença, 1974. First edition, 1959. A dictionary of Portuguese slang.

95.　Nobre, Eduardo. *Novo calão português.* Lisboa: Casa do Livro, 1979. 125 pp.
A dictionary of Portuguese slang. Includes an appendix with last-minute entries.

96.　————. *O calão: Dicionário de gíria portuguesa.* Lisboa: Casa do Livro, 1980. 159 pp.
An alphabetical dictionary of close to 5,000 Portuguese slang terms. A revised and enlarged version of no. 95. Also includes an introductory study (9–37); appendixes listing Portuguese cant, Brazilian slang, and Portuguese CB jargon; and a short bibliography.

97.　Santos, Eduardo dos, Manuel Passetti, and Fernando Cardote. *Dicionário do calão casapiano.* Lisboa: Duarte, 1976. [150 pp.]
A lexicon of the argot used by students at the Casa Pia de Lisboa.

98.　Sequeira, F. J. Martins. *Apontamentos acerca do falar do Baixo-Minho.* Lisboa: Revista de Portugal, 1957. 202 pp.
Includes a listing of Portuguese regional terms from Baixo-Minho (140–64).

99.　Silva, J. A. Capela e. *A linguagem rústica no Concelho de Elvas.* Lisboa: Revista de Portugal, 1947. 211 pp.
An inventory of the vocabulary of Portuguese rustic speech from the Concelho de Elvas with illustrative quotations taken from popular verses.

Brazil

General

100. Angenot, Jean-Pierre, Jean-Pierre Jacquemin, and Jacques L. Vincke. *Répertoire des vocables brésiliens d'origine africaine*. Lumumbashi, Zaïre: Centre de Linguistique Théorique et Appliquée, 1974. 182+ pp. A dictionary of over 1,500 Africanisms in Brazilian Portuguese. Etymological information.

101. Beaurepaire-Rohan. *Dicionário de vocábulos brasileiros*. 2nd ed. Salvador: Progresso, 1956. 244 pp. A classic study. A facsimile of the first edition (1889). Lists Brazilian popular terms.

102. Cascudo, Luís da Câmara. *Locuções tradicionais do Brasil*. Recife: Imprensa U de Pernambuco, 1970. 327 pp. The most distinguished Brazilian folklorist offers etymological remarks on more than 500 popular terms and expressions collected throughout Brazil.

103. Chamberlain, Bobby J., and Ronald M. Harmon. *A Dictionary of Informal Brazilian Portuguese (with English Index)*. Washington: Georgetown UP, 1984. 701 pp. Lists and defines approximately 7,500 terms and idioms common to informal Brazilian speech—slang, colloquialisms, figurative expressions, sports and student vocabulary, argot, and so on. Followed by an index organized from the standpoint of English. Materials are taken from interviews with Brazilian informants. Each entry includes one or more illustrative sentences. Bibliography. Over one-third of the entries have never before appeared in a dictionary.

104. Franco, Cid. *Dicionário de expressões populares brasileiras*. 3 vols. São Paulo: Editoras Unidas, 1971. Vol. 1: 479 pp.; vol. 2: 464 pp.; vol. 3: 635 pp. Includes etymologies and illustrates some of the terms and expressions with examples. Besides slang and colloquialisms, lists several items of historical, folkloric, and biblical origin. Contains an appendix with selected student terms. Bibliography.

105. Magalhães Júnior, Raymundo. *Dicionário brasileiro de provérbios, locuções e ditos curiosos, bem como de curiosidades verbais, frases feitas, ditos históricos e citações literárias, de curso corrente na língua falada e escrita*. 3rd ed. Rio de Janeiro: Documentário, 1974. 330 pp. The first edition (São Paulo: Cultrix, 1966) bears the title *Dicionário de provérbios e curiosidades, adágios comparados, frases feitas, ditos históricos e pseudo-históricos, alusões mitológicas e citações literárias de curso corrente na língua falada e escrita*. Each item is followed by an ample explanation of its origins. Entries often include parallel expressions from other languages. Bibliography.

106. Megenney, William W. "Lexical Africanisms in Bahian Portuguese." *A Bahian Heritage: An Ethnolinguistic Study of African Influences on Bahian Portuguese.* Chapel Hill: U of North Carolina, Dept. of Romance Languages, 1978. 115-61.

Includes a list of 217 lexical items of African origin found in the active or passive vocabularies of Bahian informants of various sociocultural levels.

107. Mendonça, Renato. *A influência africana no português do Brasil.* 4th ed. Rio de Janeiro: Civilização Brasileira, 1973. xv + 192 pp.

"Em convênio com o Instituto Nacional do Livro—MEC."

A classic study. In addition to analyzing the ethnographic, historical, folkloric, literary, and linguistic aspects of the topic, the work lists some 375 Brazilian terms of African origin (108-76), most of them accompanied by etymological information, indication of geographical distribution, and quotations illustrating use. Bibliography.

108. Mota, Mauro. *Os bichos na fala da gente.* Recife: Inst. J. Nabuco de Pesquisas Sociais-MEC, 1969. 235 pp.

Over 2,000 terms, expressions, and popular sayings (mainly from the Northeast) that make reference to animals. Includes an introductory study (15-61), illustrative quotations of literary origin, and a bibliography.

109. Nascentes, Antenor. *A gíria brasileira.* Rio de Janeiro: Académica, 1953. xvii + 181 pp.

A classic study written by one of the most respected Brazilian philologists. Lists approximately 3,000 words and expressions belonging to slang, underworld argot, and the jargons of various professional groups and linguistic communities. Includes many illustrative quotations and etymological observations. Bibliography.

110. ———. *Tesouro da fraseologia brasileira.* 2nd ed., corrected. Rio de Janeiro: Freitas Bastos, 1966. 316 pp.

First edition, 1945. Perhaps the most complete dictionary of modern Portuguese idioms. It lacks, however, many recent expressions.

111. Pontes, Joel. *Palavras luso-brasileiras do futebol.* Recife: Editora Universitária, 1974. 125 pp.

Introductory studies (7-37), followed by a dictionary of predominantly Brazilian soccer jargon. Based largely on interviews conducted by a team of student researchers.

112. Pugliesi, Márcio. *Dicionário de expressões idiomáticas: Locuções usuais da língua portuguesa.* São Paulo: Parma, 1981. 309 pp.

One of the best dictionaries of Brazilian Portuguese idiomatic expressions. Contains a good number of recent coinages.

113. Rector, Mônica. *A linguagem da juventude: Uma pesquisa geo-sociolingüística.* Petrópolis: Vozes, 1975. 262 pp.

"Introdução," "I. Princípios teóricos e métodos dialetológicos da geolingüística," "A. Dialetologia, lingüística, geolingüística e sociolingüística," "B. Terminologia dialetológica," "C. Metodologia dialetológica," "II. A linguagem da juventude estudantil," "A. Estudos anteriores," "B. A pesquisa," "Conclusões," "Referências Bibliográficas," "Glossário."

"O presente trabalho tem por finalidade colocar o leitor a par dos princípios teóricos e métodos da Geolingüística e mostrar a aplicação a um aspecto específico da língua portuguesa, que é a linguagem dos estudantes" (11). The glossary lists and defines approximately 900 Brazilian slang terms and expressions used by students. Not confined to strictly student jargon.

114.   Silva, Braz da. *Gíria marinheira: Como falam os homens do mar.* Rio de Janeiro: N.p., 1964. viii + 111 pp.
Nautical jargon. Includes observations and illustrative sentences for many entries.

115.   Silva, Euclides Carneiro da. *Dicionário da gíria brasileira.* Rio de Janeiro: Bloch, 1973. 217 pp.
Defines 3,000 terms and phrases belonging to the slang, argot, and popular language of contemporary Brazil. Each entry includes one or more illustrative quotations taken from novels, short stories, newspapers, and magazines. Contains an index of authors quoted and an index of publications cited.

116.   ———. *Dicionário de locuções da língua portuguesa.* Rio de Janeiro: Bloch, [1975]. 419 pp.
Lists approximately 8,000 expressions used in Brazil.

117.   Silva, Felisbelo da. *Dicionário de gíria: Gíria policial, gíria dos marginais, gíria humorística.* São Paulo: Papelivros, n.d. 112 pp.
Lists approximately 4,000 words and expressions used mainly in the underworld. Brief imaginary dialogues illustrate the use of some of them, and an appendix provides several additional recent terms. The author is a police investigator. There are several editions.

118.   Souto Maior, Mário. *Dicionário do palavrão e termos afins.* 2nd ed., rev. and enl. Recife: Guararapes, 1980. xvii + 166 pp.
A compilation of over 3,000 obscenities used in the various regions of Brazil (and Portugal). The author consulted 3,620 informants. Includes bibliographical references and some literary quotations. An appendix contains 154 additional entries. A third edition is in preparation.

119.   ———. *Dicionário folclórico da cachaça.* 3rd ed. Recife: Fundação Joaquim Nabuco, Massangana, 1985. 152 pp.
First edition, 1973. A dictionary of predominantly slang terms for *aguardente*, its consumption, and its effects. Includes an introductory study, a bibliography, and addenda.

120.   Viotti, Manuel. *Novo dicionário da gíria brasileira.* São Paulo: Bentivegna, 1956. 446 pp.
The second edition of the *Dicionário da gíria brasileira* (São Paulo: Editora

Universitária, 1945). Contains approximately 10,000 words and phrases from Brazilian popular speech (argot, professional jargons, regionalisms, idiomatic expressions). The organization and methodology leave something to be desired; nevertheless, the work is quite useful. Includes a bibliography and an appendix with Gypsy and Kimbundu (Angolan) terms.

Southeast

121. Amaral, Amadeu. *O dialeto caipira.* 3rd ed. São Paulo: HUCITEC, Secretaria da Cultura, Ciência e Tecnologia, 1976. 197 pp.
A classic study. First edition, 1920. "[E]sta edição é uma reprodução facsimilada da segunda edição publicada pelo [sic] Editora Anhembi, em 1955" (4). The first 4 parts deal with the phonetics, lexicology, morphology, and syntax of the dialect of the interior of São Paulo state. The last part (82–192) is a lexicon of selected terms.

122. Nascentes, Antenor. *O linguajar carioca.* 2nd ed., rev. Rio de Janeiro: Simões, 1953. 219 pp.
The title of the first edition is *O linguajar carioca em 1922.* The second edition is a classic study of the speech in the city of Rio de Janeiro. Situates the Brazilian and carioca dialects within the overall context of the Portuguese language, examining the carioca dialect from the standpoint of its phonology, morphology, syntax, and lexicon. Lists close to 700 regionalisms and popular terms used in the city (183–206). Bibliography.

123. Pederneiras, Raul. *Geringonça carioca: Verbetes para um dicionário de gíria.* 2nd ed., rev. and enl. Rio de Janeiro: Briguiet, 1946. 68 pp.
First edition, 1910; reprinted, 1922. A dictionary of the slang of the city of Rio de Janeiro.

124. Perdigão, Edmylson. *Linguajar da malandragem.* Rio de Janeiro: Autor, 1940. xix + 123 pp.
A lexicon of the underworld argot of Rio de Janeiro.

125. Tacla, Ariel. *Dicionário dos marginais.* 2nd ed. Rio de Janeiro: Forense-Universitária, 1981. 97 pp.
Contains more than 2,000 terms and expressions used by the criminal underworld, compiled by a former prison official in Rio de Janeiro. Preface by Carlos Lacerda, a former governor. Imaginary dialogues illustrate many entries. There are serious organizational and methodological defects. First edition, 1968. The second edition also includes an introductory study.

South

126. Corrêa, Piaguaçu. *Antigos e novos vocábulos gaúchos.* Canoas: La Salle, 1965. 105 pp.
Popular terms and expressions from the state of Rio Grande do Sul. Includes an appendix with additional entries, as well as a bibliography.

127.   *Vocabulário sul-rio-grandense.* Ed. Walter Spalding. Rio de Janeiro:
       Globo, 1964. xi + 489 pp.
A collection of terms and expressions. Incorporates the following works: Corrêa, Romaguera, *Vocabulário sul-rio-grandense*, Pelotas: Echenique, 1898, 231
pp.; Coruja, Antônio Álvares Pereira, *Coleção de vocábulos na província do Rio
Grande do Sul*, 2nd ed., London: Trübner, 1856, 32 pp.; Moraes, Luiz Carlos de,
Vocabulário sul-rio-grandense, Porto Alegre: Globo, 1935, 228 pp.; Callage, Roque, *Vocabulário gaúcho*, Porto Alegre: Globo, 1926, 143 pp.

Northeast

128.   Almeida, Horácio de. *Dicionário popular paraibano.* João Pessoa:
       Editora Universitária–U Federal da Paraíba, 1979. 180 pp.
An alphabetical listing of regionalisms from the state of Paraíba.

129.   Cabral, Tomé. *Dicionário de termos e expressões populares.* Fortaleza:
       U Federal do Ceará, 1972. 795 pp.
Records the popular vocabulary of the *sertão* of Ceará, focusing on the southern part of the state, near Cariri. Bibliography.

130.   Carneiro, Édison. *A linguagem popular da Bahia.* Rio de Janeiro, 1951.
       77 pp.
A collection of popular terms and expressions from Bahia state.

131.   Clerot, L. F. R. *Vocabulário de termos populares e gíria da Paraíba: Es-
       tudo de glotologia e semântica paraibana.* Rio de Janeiro: Riachuelo,
       1959. 102 pp.
Includes, in many cases, the etymology.

132.   Costa, F. A. Pereira da. *Vocabulário pernambucano.* 2nd ed. Recife:
       Governo do Estado de Pernambuco, Secretaria de Educação e Cultura,
       1976. 814 pp.
First edition, published posthumously, 1937. Lists and documents the popular vocabulary of Pernambuco state.

133.   Girão, Raimundo. *Vocabulário popular cearense.* Fortaleza: Imprensa U
       do Ceará, 1967. 238 pp.
Contains 3,058 entries. Lists the regionalisms of the state of Ceará. Often includes illustrative sentences or quotations and etymological notes. An introductory study of Brazilian Portuguese as distinguished from the Lusitanian variety.
Bibliography.

134.   Nonato, Raimundo. *Calepino potiguar: Gíria rio-grandense.* [Mossoró]:
       N.p., 1980. 496 pp.
A dictionary of the slang of Rio Grande do Norte state.

135.   Passos, Alexandre. *A gíria baiana.* Rio de Janeiro: São José, 1973. 102 pp.
A listing of the slang and popular terms of Salvador and Bahia state. Some entries include brief etymological notes or other documentation.

136.   Santiago, Paulino. *Dinâmica de uma linguagem: O falar de Alagoas.* Maceió: U Federal de Alagoas, 1976. 228 pp.
   The first part of the study is an essay on the popular language of the state of Alagoas (11-54). The second part, which is much more extensive, is a dictionary of popular terms and phrases. Bibliography.

137.   Seraine, Florival. *Dicionário de termos populares (registrados no Ceará).* Rio de Janeiro: Simões, 1958. 276 pp.
   "[Uma] coleção de termos de cunho marcadamente popular, usuais no Ceará, tanto em nossos dias, como em épocas passadas, os quais são, às vezes, também provincianismos lusos ou termos já registrados em léxicos portugueses, embora costumem oferecer matizes semânticos peculiares ao meio brasileiro ou regional" (5).

138.   Trigueiros, Edilberto. *A língua e o folclore da bacia do São Francisco.* Rio de Janeiro: Campanha de Defesa do Folclore Brasileiro, 1977. 191 pp.
   A dictionary of the popular speech and folklore of the São Francisco River basin.

139.   Vieira Filho, Domingos. *A linguagem popular do Maranhão.* 3rd ed., enl. São Luís: Olímpica, 1979. 105 pp.
   A listing of the popular lexicon of Maranhão state. Includes a bibliography. Second edition, 1958.

North

140.   Mendes, Amando. *Vocabulário amazônico: Estudos.* São Paulo: Soc. Impressora Brasileira, 1942. 151 pp.
   Divided into "Vocabulário amazônico relacionado com expressões usuais, peixes, pescarias, aspectos potâmicos e etnográficos" and "Termos e locuções do linguajar caboclo."

141.   Miranda, Vicente Chermont de. *Glossário paraense ou coleção de vocábulos peculiares à Amazônia e especialmente à Ilha de Marajó.* 2nd ed. Belém: U Federal do Pará, 1968. 98 pp.
   First edition, 1905. Contains approximately 500 Amazonian terms.

West-Central

142.   Ortêncio, Waldomiro Bariani. *Dicionário do Brasil central: Subsídios à filologia.* São Paulo: Ática, 1983. viii + 472 pp.
   Records the popular vocabulary of the central region of Brazil. Entries total some 14,000, many of them documented with quotations from philological studies and literature. Includes many lexical items ignored by other such studies. Contains listings of authors cited and works consulted.

Other Portuguese-Speaking Areas

Macao

143. Batalha, Graciete Nogueira. *Glossário do dialecto macaense: Notas linguísticas, etnográficas e folclóricas.* Coimbra: Revista Portuguesa de Filologia, 1977. 119–338.
An offprint of the *Revista portuguesa de filologia.* Lists the Portuguese vocabulary of Macao. Includes etymological observations.

Mozambique

144. Cabral, António. *Pequeno dicionário de Moçambique.* Lourenço Marques [Maputo]: Autor, 1972. 127 pp.
An alphabetical listing of Mozambican Portuguese regionalisms. Often notes register and region of usage. Includes addenda.

Madeira

145. Silva, Padre Fernando Augusto da. *Vocabulário popular do arquipélago da Madeira: Alguns subsídios para o seu estudo.* Funchal: Tipografia Madeira Gráfica, 1950. 149 pp.
Lists and briefly defines regionalisms from the Madeira islands.

Portuguese Literature

Current Bibliographies and Periodical Indexes

146. "Bibliografía." *Revista de filología hispánica.* See no. 3.

147. "Bibliographie." *Revue d'histoire du théâtre* 1– (1948–). Most issues contain a classified theater bibliography.

148. *Bulletin signalétique: Histoire et science de la littérature, arts du spectacle.* Paris: Centre National de la Recherche Scientifique; Centre de Documentation Sciences Humaines. Sec. C23, 1947–68; Sec. 523. 1969– . Quarterly. Annotated. Each issue includes author and subject indexes. Lists both Portuguese- and Brazilian-literature publications.

149. *MLA Directory of Periodicals.* See no. 21.

150. *MLA International Bibliography.* See no. 22.

151. "Notas bibliográficas. . . ." See no. 26.

152. *Romanische Bibliographie.* See no. 33.

153. *The Year's Work in Modern Language Studies.* See no. 39.

General Reference Works
Bibliographies

154. Foster, David W. "An Annotated Registry of Scholarly Journals in Hispanic Studies." *Revista interamericana de bibliografía* 28.2 (1978): 131–47.
    Although designed as a listing of specifically Hispanic literary journals, it does include some items devoted as well to the study of Luso-Brazilian literatures. "This is meant to be both a registry of existing journals and a guide for the placement of manuscripts" (131). Includes information on journals' editorial policies.

155. Golden, Herbert H., and Seymour O. Simches. *Modern Iberian Language and Literature: A Bibliography of Homage Studies.* See no. 16.

156. Moisés, Massaud, with the collaboration of Herti Hoeppner Ferreira, Neusa Dias Macedo, and Yara Frateschi Vieira. *Bibliografia da literatura portuguesa.* São Paulo: Saraiva–U de São Paulo, 1968. xx + 383 pp. Divided into 11 sections: "Obras gerais," "Trovadorismo," "Humanismo," "Classicismo," "Barroco," "Arcadismo," "Romantismo," "Realismo," "Simbolismo," "Modernismo," "Literatura Ultramarina."
    Each section begins with a brief listing of general critical studies and is then subdivided into genres (each of which is followed by its respective critical studies) and individual authors (with their works and respective critical bibliographies). Not annotated.

157. Valis, Noël. "Directory of Publication Sources in the Fields of Hispanic Language and Literature." See no. 37.

158. Wilgus, A. Curtis. *Latin America, Spain and Portugal: A Selected and Annotated Bibliographical Guide to Books Published in the United States, 1954–1974.* Metuchen: Scarecrow, 1977. xv + 910 pp.
    Classified and annotated. The sections on Portuguese and Brazilian culture are minimal. Portuguese fiction is mixed with that of Spain, Brazilian literature with that of other South American countries.

159. Zubatsky, David S. "A Bibliography of Cumulative Indexes to Luso-Brazilian Journals of the Nineteenth and Twentieth Centuries: Humanities and Social Sciences." See no. 40.

160. ———. "An International Bibliography of Cumulative Indexes to Journals Publishing Articles on Hispanic Languages and Literatures." See no. 42.

161. ———. "An International Bibliography of Cumulative Indices to Journals Publishing Articles on Hispanic Languages and Literatures: First Supplement." See no. 43.

Dictionaries of Authors and Biobibliographies

162. Brinches, Victor. *Dicionário biobibliográfico luso-brasileiro.* Rio de Janeiro: Fundo de Cultura, 1965. 509 pp.
    Articles include "Academias," "Arcádias," "Tendências literárias," "Autores portugueses," "Autores brasileiros."

163. Cochofel, João José, ed. *Grande dicionário da literatura portuguesa e de teoria literária.* Lisboa: Iniciativas Editoriais, 1971– .
    Published in fascicles. Volume 1 (A–Bobo). Entries cover authors, literary masterpieces, movements, and other general topics.

164.   *Columbia Dictionary of Modern European Literature.* Ed. Jean-Albert
        Bédé and William B. Edgerton. 2nd ed., rev. and enl. New York: Colum-
        bia UP, 1980. xxi + 895 pp.
    First edition, 1947. Includes articles on twentieth-century Portuguese authors
and a general article on Portuguese literature from the end of the nineteenth century to the present.

165.   Coelho, Jacinto do Prado. *Dicionário de literatura: Literatura portuguesa,
        literatura brasileira, literatura galega, estilística literária.* 3rd ed. 3 vols.
        Porto: Figueirinhas, 1973.
        Vol. 1 (A–K): 516 pp.; vol. 2 (L–S): 517–1056; vol. 3 (T–Z): 1057–526.
    A team of 45 contributors produced articles (with bibliographical data) on
authors, works, journals, topics, characters, periods, movements, genres, poetic
forms, and regions of Portuguese, Brazilian, and Galician literatures. Illustrated.
The third edition has been reprinted several times (1978, 1979, 1983); the number of volumes varies (3 or 5). The first edition, published in 1960, bears the title
Dicionário das literaturas portuguesa, galega e brasileira. The title was changed
in 1973. Currently published in 5 volumes (the fifth volume contains author and
title indexes). A monumental reference work.

166.   *Diccionario de autores iberoamericanos.* Ed. Pedro Shimose. Madrid:
        Ministerio de Asuntos Exteriores, Dirección General de Relaciones Cul-
        turales, Inst. de Cooperación Iberoamericana, 1982. 459 pp.
    Lists only writers born between 1880 and 1930. Includes some Portuguese and
Brazilian authors. Researched by a team of 7 contributors.

167.   *Encyclopedia of World Literature in the Twentieth Century.* Ed. Leonard
        S. Klein. Rev. ed. 4 vols. New York: Ungar, 1981.
        Vol. 1 (A–D): xxxv + 608 pp.; vol. 2 (E–K): xxvi + 630 pp.; vol. 3 (L–Q): xxvi
        + 619 pp.; vol. 4 (R–Z): xxx + 726 pp.
    Includes articles on Portuguese literature (3: 566–70), Brazilian literature (1:
320–24), Angolan literature (1: 95–97), Cape Verdean literature (1: 401–03),
Guinea-Bissau literature (2: 301), Mozambican literature (3: 322–24), and the literature of São Tomé and Príncipe (4: 147). Also contains articles on many individual authors, brief bibliographies of works by and about the authors, and
further reading about the literatures.

168.   Luft, Celso Pedro. *Dicionário de literatura portuguesa e brasileira.* Porto
        Alegre: Globo, 1967. 316 pp.
    A biobibliographical dictionary. Includes Portuguese and Brazilian authors as
well as literary movements.

169.   Moisés, Massaud. *A literatura portuguesa moderna: Guia biográfico,
        crítico e bibliográfico.* São Paulo: Cultrix, 1973. 202 pp.
    An alphabetical dictionary of twentieth-century Portuguese authors, written
by a team of 11 contributors. Includes biographical, critical, and bibliographical data for each author; there are also entries for various literary movements and
other general topics.

170.   Osório, João de Castro. *Ordenação crítica dos autores e obras essenciais da literatura portuguesa*. Lisboa: Império, 1947. 127 pp.
Classifies Portuguese authors by period and comments briefly on each author.

171.   *Quem é quem na literatura portuguesa*. Ed. Álvaro Manuel Machado, with the collaboration of Maria de Fátima Morna and Pedro Ferre. Lisboa: Dom Quixote, 1979. 260 pp.
Contains short articles "sobre os autores portugueses de obras de ficção, poesia ou teatro, da Idade Média aos nossos dias, incluindo locais e datas de nascimento (sempre que possível), origem social, educação e vida profissional, evolução da obra e respectiva bibliografia. . . ." Divided into two sections, "Antes de 1900" and "Depois de 1900." Followed by a short bibliography and a brief appendix that defines terms referring to literary periods and movements. Includes some Luso-African authors.

172.   Seymour-Smith, Martin. *The New Guide to Modern World Literature*. 3rd ed. New York: Bedrick, 1985. xxviii + 1,396 pp.
First edition, 1973. Includes articles on Portuguese authors (1026-35) and Brazilian authors (955-72) of the twentieth century. Index of authors, literary movements and terms, and titles of books.

173.   Silva, Inocêncio Francisco da. *Dicionario bibliographico portuguez: Estudos aplicaveis a Portugal e ao Brasil*. Lisboa: Nacional, 1858-1958. 23 vols.
Vols. 1-7: A-Z; vols. 8-20 (1-3, supp.): A-Z, 1867-1911; vols. 14-15: Luís de Camões; vol. 21: Alexandre Herculano; Vol. 22: A-Au; vol. 23: Soares, Ernesto, *Guia bibliográfica*, Coimbra: Biblioteca da Universidade, 1958, xxviii + 762 pp.; A-Z (1923-58). Vols. 10-22 rev. and enl. by Brito Aranha.
A biobibliography organized according to the first names of the authors. Lists books published in the eighteenth and nineteenth centuries. See also Fonseca, Martinho Augusto Ferreira da, *Aditamentos ao* Dicionário bibliográfico português *de Inocêncio Francisco da Silva*, Coimbra: Imprensa da Universidade, 1927, 337 pp.; Souza, José Soares de, *Índice alfabético do* Dicionário bibliográfico português *de Inocêncio Francisco da Silva*, [São Paulo]: Dept. de Cultura, Div. de Bibliotecas, 1938, 264 pp.; Carmo, Célio Assis do, "Índice brasileiro do *Dicionário bibliográfico português* de Inocêncio Francisco da Silva," *Revista do livro* 9 (1958): 235-51; 10 (1958): 231-48.

Genres

Theater

174.   Pereira, Benjamim Enes. *Bibliografia analítica de etnografia portuguesa*. See no. 27.

175.   Rebello, Luiz Francisco. *Dicionário do teatro português*. Lisboa: Prelo, 1968- .
According to the "Nota prévia," the *Dicionário* is not limited to listing authors

of theatrical texts; it also includes "dramaturgos, comediantes, encenadores, compositores, cenógrafos, arquitectos e decoradores, empresários, críticos, historiógrafos e teorizadores de estética teatral, e ainda obras, temas, correntes, movimentos e tendências, géneros e formas teatrais, edifícios, companhias e publicações teatrais, conexões do teatro com as outras artes," and so on. Illustrated.

176.   Révah, I. S. "Bibliographie des travaux sur l'histoire du théâtre portugais parus de 1947 à 1950." *Bulletin d'histoire du théâtre portugais* 2 (1951): 107-12.
"Avant Gil Vicente," "Gil Vicente," "De Gil Vicente à Garrett," "De Garrett à nos jours," "Etudes spéciales."
There is also a supplement in the same issue: Reis, J. E. Morgado, "Supplément à la 'Bibliographie des travaux sur l'histoire du théâtre portugais parus de 1947 à 1950.' " *Bulletin d'histoire du théâtre portugais* 2 (1951): 255-59.

Reference Works Dealing with Particular Periods, Authors, or Works

Middle Ages

General

177.   *Bibliografia geral portuguesa: Século XV.* 2 vols. Lisboa: Academia das Ciências de Lisboa, 1941-44.
Vol. 1: ci + 402 pp.; vol. 2: cxiv + 832 pp.
A well-documented and richly illustrated bibliography. Contains several indexes.

178.   Cintra, Maria Adelaide Valle. *Bibliografia de textos medievais portugueses.* 2nd ed., rev. and enl. Lisboa: Centro de Estudos Filológicos, 1960. 78 pp.
A classified bibliography. Contents: "Poesia," "Novelística," "Literatura religiosa, Regras monásticas," "História," "Viagens, epístolas, oratória, etc.," "Prosa moralística," "Textos jurídicos," "Tratados técnicos," "Dissertações de licenciatura," "Aditamento," "Índice de autores e de títulos de obras de autor desconhecido," "Índice onomástico dos editores de textos, autores de glossários, críticos, etc."

179.   Machado, Diogo Barbosa. *Biblioteca lusitana, histórica, crítica e cronológica.* 4 vols. Coimbra: Atlântida, 1965-67.
A reprint of the first edition (Lisboa, 1741-59). A biobibliographical work on Portuguese authors that covers from the origins of Portuguese literature to the middle of the eighteenth century. Organized according to the first names of authors. See also Gusmão, F. A. Rodrigues de, *Apontamentos para a continuação da Biblioteca lusitana,* Coimbra: Instituto, 1958.

180.   Tavani, Giuseppe. "I più recenti studi italiani sulla letteratura portoghese medievale." *Anuario de estudios medievales* 3 (1966): 565–73.
A bibliographical essay. Lists Portuguese medieval studies published by Italian scholars during the first half of the sixties.

Festschriften Index

181.   Williams, Harry Franklin. *An Index of Medieval Studies Published in Festschriften.* . . . See no. 38.

Arthurian Legends

182.   *Bulletin bibliographique de la Société Internationale Arthurienne.* 1– (1949–).
A current bibliography. Includes Portuguese literature. Organized by country of publication.

183.   Sharrer, Harvey L. *A Critical Bibliography of Hispanic Arthurian Materials.* Vol. 1: *Texts. The Prose Romance Cycles.* Research Bibliographies and Check Lists 3. London: Grant, 1977. 55 pp.
"Included in this volume are the prose romances of the Vulgate, Post-Vulgate and Tristan cycles; that is, the surviving manuscripts and early printed editions, together with modern editions and reviews thereof" (10).

Ballads

184.   Armistead, Samuel G. "A Critical Bibliography of the Hispanic Ballad in Oral Tradition." *El romancero hoy: Historia, comparatismo, bibliografía crítica.* Ed. Samuel G. Armistead, Diego Catalán, and Antonio Sánchez Romeralo. Madrid: Gredos–Cátedra Seminario Menéndez Pidal, 1979. 3: 199–310.
A critical, annotated bibliography. Lists publications appearing between 1971 and 1978, as well as those that appeared earlier but were reviewed after 1971.

Galician-Portuguese Poetry

185.   Pellegrini, Silvio, and Giovanna Marroni. *Nuovo repertorio bibliografico della prima lirica galego-portoghese (1814–1977).* L'Aquila: Japadre, 1981. 197 pp.
Marroni's updating of the *Repertorio bibliografico della prima lirica galego-portoghese* published by Silvio Pellegrini in 1939. Represents a considerable expansion of the listings.

Cantigas d'escárnio e maldizer

186.   Lapa, Manuel Rodrigues. *Vocabulário galego-português tirado da edição crítica das cantigas d'escarnho e de mal dizer.* Vigo: Galaxia, 1965. 108 pp.
A Galician-Portuguese glossary of the the *cantigas d'escárnio e maldizer* published by Rodrigues Lapa in a separate Galaxia volume in 1965.

A demanda do Santo Graal

187.   Magne, Augusto. *Glossário da* Demanda do Santo Graal. 3 vols.? Rio de Janeiro: Inst. Nacional do Livro, 1967– .
Vol. 1 (A–D): vii + 436 pp.
Original edition: A demanda do Santo Graal: *Vol. 3. Glossário.* Rio de Janeiro: Nacional, 1944. 455 pp. Magne died in 1966.

Authors

Dom Duarte

188.   Palhano, Herbert. *A expressão léxico-gramatical do* Leal conselheiro. 2nd ed., enl. Lisboa: Revista de Portugal, 1949. 183 pp.
First edition, 1945. The study mainly defines and comments on the work's vocabulary.

Gil Vicente

189.   Azevedo, Luísa Maria de Castro. *Bibliografia vicentina.* Lisboa: Biblioteca Nacional, 1942. xii + 1,003 pp.
Contents: "Obras originais," "Traduções, paráfrases e adaptações," "Análise," "Cenas várias e excerptos," "Bibliografia vicentina," "Escola vicentina," "Escola clássica, italiana ou mirandina," "Algumas obras sobre Gil Vicente, Sá de Miranda, suas escolas e fontes inspiradoras," "Renascimento e humanismo," "Antologias, crestomatias, enciclopédias e outras obras," "Teatro," "Suplemento," "Índice das publicações periódicas," "Índice das obras de Gil Vicente por ordem da data, em parte provável do seu aparecimento," "Índice didascálico e de referências," "Índice onomástico e de referências."
Lists 3,175 works.

190.   Comissão Nacional do V Centenário de Gil Vicente. *Exposições vicentinas: Catálogo.* Lisboa: Ministério da Educação Nacional, 1965. 143 pp.
Contents: "Biblioteca Geral da Universidade de Coimbra," "Biblioteca Pública Municipal do Porto," "Biblioteca Municipal de Santarém," "Biblioteca Pública de Évora."

191.   Stathatos, Constantine Christopher. *A Gil Vicente Bibliography (1940–1975).* London: Grant, 1980. 132 pp.
Contents: "Bibliographic Sources," "Editions and Adaptations," "Translations," "Critical Studies," "Index of Scholars and Translators," "Subject Index." See also the supplement: Stathatos, C. C., "Supplement to *A Gil Vicente Bibliography (1940–1975),*" *Segismundo* 35–36 (1982): 9–17. Contains 108 entries.

Classical Period

General Bibliographies and Library Catalogs

192.   Fédération Internationale des Sociétés et Institut pour l'Etude de la Renaissance. *Bibliographie internationale de l'humanisme et de la Renaissance, travaux parus en 1965–.* Genève: Droz, 1966–.
A current bibliography. Volumes 1–6 are organized alphabetically by author and contain a subject index. Beginning with volume 7 (1971), each volume is divided into 2 parts, "Personnages et oeuvres anonymes" and "Matières." Each volume contains an author index. Lists books, articles, new editions, and translations of European Renaissance authors. Thorough.

193.   Goldsmith, V. F. *A Short Title Catalogue of Spanish and Portuguese Books, 1601–1700, in the Library of the British Museum (The British Library—Reference Section).* Folkestone: Dawsons, 1974. 250 pp.
An alphabetical catalog of the British Museum's seventeenth-century Spanish and Portuguese holdings.

194.   "Literature of the Renaissance." *Studies in Philology* 36–66 (1939–69).
The most comprehensive current Renaissance bibliography published during the period indicated. Includes book reviews.

Sermons

195.   Horch, Rosemarie Erika. *Sermões impressos dos autos da fé: Bibliografia.* Rio de Janeiro: Biblioteca Nacional, 1969. 123 pp.
A bibliography of the published sermons for autos-da-fé occurring in Portugal and Goa during the seventeenth and eighteenth centuries.

Authors

Luís Vaz de Camões

196.   Martins, António Coimbra. *IV Centenario de Os lusíadas de Camões, 1572–1972.* Madrid: Biblioteca Nacional de Madrid; Fundación Calouste Gulbenkian, 1972. xxvi + 358 pp.
Contents: "Manuscritos," "Ediciones, traducciones y adaptaciones de *Os lusíadas,*" "Sobre Camões y *Os lusíadas,*" "Influencias y proyección de *Os lusíadas*

en Portugal," "Camões y España: Reseña cronológica," "Camões y España: Géneros literarios y sectores bibliográficos," "Índices de nombres propios." A bibliographical catalog of the exposition. Annotated.

197.　Mesquita, Esmeralda Ribeiro de. *Camoniana: Catálogo coletivo da cidade do Rio de Janeiro.* Rio de Janeiro: Biblioteca Nacional, 1972. 138 pp.

Contents: "Obras completas," *"Os lusíadas,"* "Lírica," "Teatro," "Cartas," "Obras em periódicos (números especiais)," "Índice das bibliotecas."

Includes 502 titles found in 35 libraries, institutes, and cultural centers.

198.　Cunha, A. G. *Índice analítico do vocabulário de* Os lusíadas. 3 vols. Rio de Janeiro: Inst. Nacional do Livro, Ministério da Educação e Cultura, 1966.

Vol. A (lxix + c. 400 pp.): "Introdução e Fac-Símiles" [da primeira edição, de 1572]; vol. B (450 pp.): A–I; vol. C (442 pp.): J–Z.

An alphabetical index of the vocabulary in the epic poem. Indicates the passages in which each item occurs.

199.　Nogueira, Júlio. *Dicionário e gramática de* Os lusíadas. Rio de Janeiro: Freitas Bastos, 1960. 438 pp.

"Inclui topônimos, antropônimos, astrônimos e mitônimos. Estudo sobre as formas de linguagem do tempo de Camões."

An alphabetical dictionary. Lists and comments on the toponyms, anthroponyms, and so on, as well as the grammatical peculiarities of the poem (e.g., verbal agreement, irregular syntax).

200.　Verdelho, Telmo. *Índice reverso de* Os lusíadas. Coimbra: Biblioteca Geral da Universidade, 1981. xxiii + 438 pp.

An alphabetical index of the vocabulary of the epic poem arranged according to the last letter of each word. Also indicates the textual location of each entry.

António da Fonseca Soares

201.　Pontes, Maria de Lourdes. *Bibliografia de António da Fonseca Soares (Frei António das Chagas).* Lisboa: Centro de Estudos Filológicos, 1950. 127 pp.

Divided into "Obras manuscritas" and "Obras impressas."

Eighteenth Century

Folhetos

202.　Horch, Rosemarie Erika. *Catálogo dos folhetos da Coleção Barbosa Machado.* Rio de Janeiro: Biblioteca Nacional, 1974– .

An annotated bibliography of the *folhetos* in the Barbosa Machado Collection written by eighteenth-century Portuguese authors. The several published sections together constitute volume 92 of the *Anais da Biblioteca Nacional.*

Nineteenth Century

General Bibliography

203.   Elkins, A. C., Jr., and L. S. Forstner, eds. *The Romantic Movement Bibliography, 1936–1970.* . . . 7 vols. Ann Arbor: Pierian, 1973.
Volume 7 includes 5 indexes: author or main entry, reviewer, subject, person as subject, and category.

Authors

Almeida Garrett

204.   Lima, Henrique de Campos Ferreira. *Inventário do espólio literário de Garrett.* Coimbra: Biblioteca Geral da Universidade, 1948. 107 pp.
Contents: "Obras manuscritas de Garrett," "Obras de Garrett impressas," "Ciências e negócios públicos."
Lists the holdings of Almeida Garrett's personal library.

Alexandre Herculano

205.   Biblioteca Pública Municipal do Porto. *Alexandre Herculano: Exposição bibliográfica comemorativa do I centenário da sua morte, 1877–1977.* Porto, 1977. 231 pp.
Contents: "Bibliografia de Alexandre Herculano," "Cartas de Alexandre Herculano," "Bibliografia sobre Alexandre Herculano," "Documentação," "Reproduções fotográficas e outras," "Apêndice à Bibliografia sobre Alexandre Herculano," "Extras."
A catalog of the library's collection.

Camilo Castelo Branco

206.   Felgueiras, A. *Camiliana I: Catálogo das obras originais de Camilo Castelo Branco, 1845–1971.* Porto: Vale Formoso, 1972. xi + 511 pp.
Contents: "Das obras originais . . . ," "Das gravuras," "Das obras originais—ordem cronológica."
A detailed descriptive bibliography of the various editions of Camilo's fiction.

Eça de Queiroz

207.   Da Cal, Ernesto Guerra. *Lengua y estilo de Eça de Queiroz. Apéndice: Bibliografía queirociana sistemática y anotada e iconografía artística del hombre y la obra.* 3 vols. Coimbra: U de Coimbra, 1975.
Vol. 1, *Bibliografía activa (fuentes primarias)*: 662 pp.; vol. 2, *Bibliografía pasiva*

(fuentes secundarias): 2 pts., 1,207 pp.; vol. 3, *Obras artísticas derivadas de la figura y de la creación de Eça de Queiroz*: 614 pp.

The most complete and learned Queirosian bibliography to date. The author regards it as the appendix to his book *Lengua y estilo de Eça de Queiroz*, published in 1954. Annotations and other remarks in Spanish. The second volume lists 8,862 critical studies.

208. "Eça de Queiroz: Subsídios para a sua bíblio-iconografia." *Eça de Queiroz: In memoriam*. Ed. Eloy do Amaral and M. Cardoso Martha. 2nd ed., enl. Coimbra: Atlântida, 1977. 419–514.

Contents: "Eça de Queiroz escreveu sozinho," "Escreveu com Ramalho Ortigão," "Dirigiu," "Prefaciou," "Traduziu," "Colaborou em," "Traduções das suas obras. Outras traduções," "A obra de Eça no teatro," "Estudos sobre a sua vida e obra," "Estudos sobre Eça de Queiroz (sem nome de autor), insertos em enciclopédias, dicionários, revistas e jornais," "Epistolário," "Iconografia," "Sessões solenes comemorativas do primeiro centenário. Conferências. Homenagens e comemorações," "Exposições," "Vária."

209. Reis, Antônio Simões dos. *Eça de Queiroz no Brasil*. Rio de Janeiro: Valverde, 1945. 103 pp.

A bibliography of critical studies on Eça published in Brazil. Lists 425 works. Some annotations.

210. Sá, Victor de. *Bibliografia queirosiana*. Braga: Minerva, 1945. 77 pp.

Contents: "Panorâmica do livro em Portugal" (essay), "Quadro cronológico," "Universalidade de Eça de Queiroz," "Obras sobre Eça," "Estudos queirosianos insertos em revistas," "Homenagens a Eça de Queiroz," "A arte perpétua de Eça."

211. Albuquerque, Paulo de Medeiros. *Dicionário de tipos e personagens de Eça de Queiroz*. São Paulo: MM; Brasília: Inst. Nacional do Livro, 1977. 156 pp.

An alphabetical inventory of Queirosian characters. Each entry situates the character and contains a quotation about him or her.

212. Catton, Albano Pereira. *Eça de Queiroz: Dicionário biográfico dos seus personagens*. [Rio de Janeiro]: Borsoi, n.d. 488 pp.

Contains an entry for each of Eça's main characters. An index of secondary characters directs the reader to main-character entries in which the secondary characters are mentioned.

Twentieth Century

Authors

Fernando Pessoa

213. Blanco, José. *Fernando Pessoa: Esboço de uma bibliografia*. [Lisboa]: Nacional; Moeda; Centro de Estudos Pessoanos, 1983. 482 pp.

Divided into "Bibliografia activa," "Bibliografia passiva" (1,312 studies), and "Traduções." The most extensive bibliography of Pessoa's works published to date.

214.	Galvão, José. *Fontes impressas da obra de Fernando Pessoa: Investigação.* Lisboa: Santelmo, [1968]. 118 pp.
Contents: "Colaboração em revistas," "Colaboração em jornais e revistas," "Poemas ingleses e um poema inédito," "Tábua bibliográfica das suas traduções de livros de carácter religioso."

215.	Iannone, Carlos Alberto. *Bibliografia de Fernando Pessoa.* 2nd ed., rev. and enl. São Paulo: Quíron; Brasília: Inst. Nacional do Livro, 1975. xvii + 84 pp.
Contents: "Bibliografia de Fernando Pessoa," "Bibliografia da crítica sobre Fernando Pessoa," and an index. The bibliography of critical studies lists 681 items. Not annotated.

Stylistics

216.	Hatzfeld, Helmut. *Bibliografía crítica de la nueva estilística aplicada a las literaturas románicas.* Madrid: Gredos, 1955.

217.	———. "Spain and Portugal." *A Critical Bibliography of the New Stylistics Applied to the Romance Literature 1900–1952.* University of North Carolina Studies in Comparative Literature 5. Chapel Hill: [U of North Carolina P], 1953. 64–65, 225–26.

218.	———. "Portuguese and Luso-American Literature." *A Critical Bibliography of the New Stylistics Applied to the Romance Literature 1953–1965.* University of North Carolina Studies in Comparative Literature 37. Chapel Hill: [U of North Carolina P], 1966. 119–21.

219.	———. "Stilische Studien in Portugal und Brasilien." *Aufsätze zur portugiesischen Kulturgeschichte* 1 (1961): 203–20.

Bibliographies of Translations
General

220.	*Index Translationum.* Quarterly, os 1–31. Paris: Inst. of International Cooperation, 1932–40. Annual, ns 1– (1948–). Paris: UNESCO, 1949– .
Now an annual. Lists book-length translations for most countries. Normally includes original title in listing.

221. *Yearbook of Comparative and General Literature.* Chapel Hill. 1–19 (1952–70).
   With the publication in 1961 of volume 10, covering 1960, the *Yearbook* initiated an annual bibliography of works in English translation published in the United States. A list of book-length translations alternates with a list of translations published in periodicals and journals. Organized according to language.

222. Sader, Marion. *Comprehensive Index to English Language Little Magazines 1890–1970.* 8 vols. Millwood: Kraus, 1976.
   Lists articles and works of creative writing (including those translated from other languages) published in 100 literary journals.

Portugal

223. Berrien, William, Alfred Hower, Gerald M. Moser, and Marion A. Zeitlin. "Portuguese Literature." [Rev. by Benjamin M. Woodbridge, Jr.] *The Romance Literatures. A Bibliography.* Vol. 3 of *The Literatures of the World in English Translation.* 3 vols. Ed. George B. Parks and Ruth Z. Temple. New York: Ungar, 1967–70. 3.1: 171–91.
   A classified, annotated bibliography of works of and about Portuguese literature translated into English. Divided into: "Background," "Literary Studies," "Collections," "Early Period: Thirteenth to Sixteenth Centuries: Individual Authors," "Seventeenth and Eighteenth Centuries: Individual Authors," "Nineteenth and Twentieth Centuries: Individual Authors."

224. Estorninho, Carlos. "Portuguese Literature in English Translation." *Portugal and Brazil: An Introduction.* Ed. H. V. Livermore. Oxford: Clarendon, 1963. 129–38.
   An unannotated chronological bibliography of works of Portuguese literature translated into English between 1653 and 1950.

225. Horn-Monval, Madeleine. *Répertoire bibliographique des traductions et adaptations françaises du théâtre étranger du xvème siècle à nos jours.* Paris: Centre National de la Recherche Scientifique, 1958–   .
   Vol. 4: "Théâtre espagnol," "Théâtre de l'Amérique Latine," "Théâtre portugais."

226. Siebenmann, Gustav, and Donatella Casetti. *Bibliographie der aus dem Spanischen, Portugiesischen, und Katalanischen ins Deutsche übersetzten Literatur (1945–1983).* Tübingen: Niemeyer, 1985. xx + 190 pp.
   Includes a listing of German-language translations of works written originally in Portuguese.

227. Solver, Loretta. "Brazil and Portugal." *Women Writers in Translation: An Annotated Bibliography, 1945–82.* Garland Reference Library of the Humanities 228. New York: Garland, 1984. 5–8.
   Lists only works in translation. Each item is briefly discussed. Includes biographical material and information on the quality of particular translations. Introduction.

Comparative Literature and Cross-Cultural Scholarship

General

228.   Baldensperger, Fernand, and Werner P. Friedrich. *Bibliography of Comparative Literature.* University of North Carolina Studies in Comparative Literature 1. Chapel Hill: [U of North Carolina P], 1950. xxiv + 701 pp.
A classified bibliography. Comprehensive, but bibliographical data are often not complete, and the volume lacks an index.

229.   *Yearbook of Comparative and General Literature.* See no. 221.

Portugal

230.   Gyberg, Erik. *Portugal i svensk litteratur: En bibliografi.* Acta Bibliothecae Universitatis Gothoburgensis 17. Göteborg: Universitetsbibliotek, 1975. xii + 77 pp.
"Nesta bibliografia estão incluídos livros e artigos sobre Portugal publicados na Suécia até 1970. A bibliografia contém literatura sueca sobre Portugal, literatura portuguesa traduzida para o sueco e também as obras estrangeiras traduzidas para sueco, versando um tema português" (vii).

231.   Rogers, Francis M., and David T. Haberly. *Brazil, Portugal and Other Portuguese-Speaking Lands: A List of Books Primarily in English.* See no. 31.

Bibliographies of Dissertations

United States

General

232.   *Microfilm Abstracts* 1-11 (1938-51); *Dissertation Abstracts* 12-29 (1952-June 1969); *Dissertation Abstracts International* 30- (July 1969-).
Abstracts of approximately 500 words each describe the dissertations cataloged. The work was divided into 2 sections with volume 27: (A) Humanities and Social Sciences and (B) Sciences and Engineering. In 1977, a third section was added that includes abstracts of dissertations from many West European universities. Several indexes.

Hispanic and Luso-Brazilian

233. Chatham, James R., and Enrique Ruiz-Fornells. *Dissertations in Hispanic Languages and Literatures: An Index of Dissertations Completed in the United States and Canada, 1876-1966.* Lexington: UP of Kentucky, 1970. xiv + 120 pp.
Organized by author and subject within chronological periods. Includes an index of dissertation authors. Lists American and Canadian dissertations on Portuguese, Brazilian, Spanish, Spanish American, Catalan, and Galician literary topics and on Portuguese, Spanish, Catalan, and Galician languages.

234. Chatham, James R., and Carmen C. McClendon. *Dissertations in Hispanic Languages and Literatures: An Index of Dissertations Completed in the United States and Canada. Vol. 2, 1967-77.* Lexington: UP of Kentucky, 1981. xi + 162 pp.
Arranged by dissertation author. Includes a detailed author and subject index. Besides indexing the types of materials included in volume 1 (no. 233), contains "a retrospective listing of dissertations on the teaching and learning of Catalan, Portuguese, and Spanish as well as those written on bilingualism involving these languages with other tongues" (vii).

235. Hanson, Carl A. "Dissertations on Luso-Brazilian Topics: A Bibliography of Dissertations Completed in the United States, Great Britain and Canada, 1892-1970." *Americas: A Quarterly Review of Inter-American Cultural History* 30.2 (1973): 251-67; 30.3 (1974): 373-403.
"I. Portugal," "A. Reference," "B. General and Miscellaneous," "C. Medieval Portugal (to ca. 1500)," "D. Imperial Portugal, ca. 1500-1800," "E. Nineteenth and Twentieth Century Portugal," "II. The Portuguese Empire," "A. Portuguese Africa," "B. The Portuguese in Asia," "C. Colonial Brazil," "D. The Rio de la Plata Region (to ca. 1850)," "III. Brazil," "A. Reference," "B. General and Miscellaneous," "C. Royalty in Brazil, 1808-1889," "D. Republican Brazil, 1889-1945," "E. Brazil since World War II," "1. Anthropology, Archaeology and Indigenous Languages," "2. Business Administration," "3. Economics," "4. Education," "5. Geography," "6. History," "7. Journalism and Mass Communications," "8. Language and Literature," "9. Music," "10. Political Science," "11. Religion," "12. Social Psychology, Social Work and Sociology," "Addendum," "Selected List of Sources Consulted."
Lists all US, British, and Canadian dissertations on Luso-Brazilian subjects during the designated period.

236. *Hispania.* Quarterly. American Assn. of Teachers of Spanish and Portuguese, 1918- .
In its May issue, *Hispania* has for many years published a list of Hispanic and Luso-Brazilian literature and language doctoral dissertations completed and in progress at US and Canadian universities. Currently classified by literature or, for linguistics dissertations, by language. There is a further breakdown into genres or, for linguistics, into "applied" or "historical." Various compilers; currently prepared by Howard M. Fraser.

237.   *Modern Language Journal.* Quarterly. Natl. Federation of Modern Language Teachers Organizations, 1916– .
Also publishes an annual list; not as useful to Luso-Brazilianists, however, as the *Hispania* list (no. 236). Includes only dissertations completed in the previous year.

238.   Chatham, James R., and Carmen C. McClendon. "Dissertations in Medieval Hispanic Languages and Literatures Accepted in the United States and Canada, 1967–1976." *La corónica* 6 (1978): 97–103; 7 (1979): 43–50.

239.   Tate, R. Brian, et al. "Bibliography of Doctoral Dissertations on Themes of Medieval Peninsular Literature." *La corónica* 6 (1978): 26–37.
Includes works in progress and titles begun or completed between 1974 and the end of 1976. Arranged by author.

Western Europe

240.   Chatham, James R., and Sara Matthews Scales. *Western European Dissertations on the Hispanic and Luso-Brazilian Languages and Literatures: A Retrospective Index.* [Mississippi State U, Dept. of Foreign Languages, 1984]. xiii + 145 pp.
Lists 6,050 dissertations prepared through 1981. Arranged by dissertation author. Detailed subject index.

France

241.   Fichier Central des Thèses, 200 av. de la République, U de Paris X, Nanterre, France.
Holdings include a file of 50,000 dissertations in progress and 20,000 dissertations that have been completed since 1970. See James R. Chatham, "Bibliographic Control of Doctoral Dissertations in France," *Hispania* 65 (1982): 109.

Germany and Austria

242.   Flasche, Hans. *Romance Languages and Literature as Presented in German Doctoral Dissertations, 1885–1950.* Charlottesville: Bibliographical Soc. of the U of Virginia, 1958.
Items 4669–83 refer to Luso-Brazilian dissertations.

243.   Rodríguez Richart, José. "*Habilitationsschriften* y tesis de doctorado realizadas en las universidades de Austria, de la República Democrática Alemana y de la República Federal de Alemania, sobre temas de lengua y literatura española y portuguesa (1945–1974)." *Iberoromania* ns 3 (1975): 205–25.

244.   "Die romanistischen Dissertationen." *Romanistisches Jahrbuch* 4– (1951–).

A current annual list of German and Austrian doctoral dissertations. Arranged by university.

United Kingdom and Ireland

245.   Jones, C. A. "Theses in Hispanic Studies Approved for Higher Degrees by British Universities to 1971." *Bulletin of Hispanic Studies* 49 (1972): 325-54.

246.   Hodcroft, F. W. "Theses in Hispanic Studies Approved for Higher Degrees by British and Irish Universities (1972-1974) (with Some Additional Earlier Titles)." *Bulletin of Hispanic Studies* 52 (1975): 325-44.

247.   Mackenzie, D. "Theses in Hispanic Studies Approved for Higher Degrees by British and Irish Universities (1975-1978) (with Some Additional Earlier Titles)." *Bulletin of Hispanic Studies* 56 (1979): 283-304.

248.   Johnson, M. "Theses in Hispanic Studies Approved for Higher Degrees by British and Irish Universities (1979-1982) (with Some Additional Earlier Titles)." *Bulletin of Hispanic Studies* 61 (1984): 235-61.
   Organized by dissertation author. Pages 235-39 pertain to Hispanic and Luso-Brazilian languages and literatures.

National Bibliographies

249.   *Arquivo de bibliografia portuguesa.* Coimbra: Atlântida, 1955- .
   Devoted to the publication of bibliographical studies on a variety of topics.

250.   *Boletim internacional de bibliografia luso-brasileira.* Lisboa: Fundação Calouste Gulbenkian, 1960-73.
   Subject varies. See especially the section entitled "Registo bibliográfico."

251.   Lisboa. Biblioteca Nacional. *Boletim de bibliografia portuguesa.* Lisboa: Biblioteca Nacional, 1935- . Vols. 1-17: 1935-51; vols. 21-30: 1955-64; vols. 39- : 1973- .
   A classified current bibliography of Portuguese publications.

252.   Lisboa. Biblioteca Nacional. *Repertório das publicações periódicas portuguesas.* Lisboa: Biblioteca Nacional. 1964- .
   A classified current bibliography of Portuguese periodicals. The first supplement is for 1961; there are others.

253.   *Livros de Portugal.* Boletim Mensal do Grémio Nacional dos Editores e Livreiros.
   A current bibliography, presently trimestral. Represents a selection from the *Boletim de bibliografia portuguesa* published by the Biblioteca Nacional (no. 251).

254. *Periódicos portugueses de ciências, letras e artes.* 1st ser. Lisboa: Inst. para a Alta Cultura, 1946- .
A classified current bibliography of scientific, literary, and artistic journals published in Portugal.

Union Lists and Library and Collection Catalogs

General

United States

255. *Library of Congress Catalog . . . Books: Subjects 1950-54.* 20 vols. 1955; *1955-59.* 22 vols. 1960; *1960-64.* 25 vols. 1965; *1965-69.* 42 vols. 1970; *1970-74.* 100 vols. 1976.
A subject guide to Library of Congress acquisitions. Published quarterly and in yearly and 5-year cumulations.

256. *The National Union Catalog, Pre-1956 Imprints: A Cumulative Author List Representing Library of Congress Printed Cards and Titles Reported by Other American Libraries.* . . . 685 vols. [London]: Mansell, 1968-80. Supp. vol. 686- (1980-).

257. *The National Union Catalog. 1958-62.* 50 vols. New York: Rowman, 1963; *1963-67.* 59 vols. Ann Arbor: Edwards, 1969; *1968-72.* 104 vols. Ann Arbor: Edwards, 1973; *1973-77.* 135 vols. Totowa: Rowman, 1978.
The *NUC* is one of the most comprehensive and accurate listings of bibliographical data on worldwide publications. It indexes the book holdings of major US and Canadian public, university, and other libraries. Published monthly and in quarterly, yearly, and 5-year cumulative listings.

258. *Union List of Serials in Libraries of the United States and Canada.* 3rd ed. Ed. Edna Brown Titus. 4 vols. New York: Wilson, 1965.

259. *New Serials Titles: A Union List of Serials Commencing Publication after December 31, 1949. 1950-70 Cumulation.* 4 vols. Washington: Library of Congress; New York: Bowker, 1973. *1971-75 Cumulation.* 2 vols. Washington: Library of Congress, 1976; *1976-79 Cumulation.* 2 vols. Washington: Library of Congress, 1980.
The union catalogs of serials are the most comprehensive listings of serial publications found in the libraries of the United States and Canada.

France

260. Bibliothèque Nationale. *Catalogue général des livres imprimés: Auteurs.* 231 vols. Paris: Imprimerie Nationale, 1897-1981.

261. ———. *Catalogue général des livres imprimés: Auteurs, collectivités-auteurs, anonymes, 1960–1964.* 12 vols. Paris: Imprimerie Nationale, 1965–67.

262. ———. *Catalogue général des livres imprimés: Auteurs, collectivités-auteurs, anonymes, 1960–1969.* Ser. 1: Caractères latins. 1– . Paris: Imprimerie Nationale, 1972– .
Catalogs of the French National Library.

263. ———. Département des Périodiques. *Catalogue collectif des périodiques du début du xviiième siècle à 1939.* 5 vols. Paris: Imprimerie Nationale, 1967–82.
A catalog of about 75,000 French and foreign serial publications found in the Bibliothèque Nationale and 70 other large French libraries.

Spain

264. Madrid. Ministerio de Cultura. Dirección General del Libro y Biblioteca. *Catálogo colectivo de publicaciones periódicas en bibliotecas españolas: 5. Humanidades, II. Lingüística y literatura.* Madrid: Inst. Bibliográfico Hispánico, 1979. lvii + 693 pp.
Indexes philological, linguistic, and literary journals found in 525 Spanish libraries.

United Kingdom

265. British Museum. *General Catalogue of Printed Books.* Photolithographic ed. to 1955. 263 vols. London: Trustees of the British Museum, 1959–66.

266. ———. *General Catalogue of Printed Books.* 10-year supp. 1956–65. 50 vols. London: Trustees of the British Museum, 1968.
A catalog of the British Museum Library.

267. *British Union-Catalog of Periodicals. . . .* Ed. James D. Stewart, Muriel E. Hammond, and Erwin Saenger. 4 vols. New York: Academic, 1955–58. Cont.: *Supplement to 1960.* New York: Academic, 1962. 991 pp. *New Periodical Titles, 1960–1968, 1969–1973.* 2 vols. London: Butterworths, 1970–76. *New Periodical Titles, 1974–* . London: Butterworths, 1974– .
The British counterpart to *Union List of Serials* (no. 258).

Portugal

United States

General

268.   Downs, Robert B. "Spanish, Portuguese and Latin American Literature."
        American Library Resources. Chicago: American Library Assn., 1950.
        247–48.

269.   ———. "Spanish, Portuguese and Latin American Literature." *American Library Resources.* Supp. 1950–61. Chicago: American Library Assn.,
        1962. 126–27.

270.   ———. "Spanish, Portuguese and Latin American Literature." *American Library Resources.* Supp. 1961–70. Chicago: American Library Assn.,
        1972. 127–28.

271.   ———. "Spanish, Portuguese and Latin American Literature." *American Library Resources.* Supp. 1971–80. Chicago: American Library Assn.,
        1981. 94–95.

The Downs bibliographies (nos. 268–71) supply information on Hispanic and
Luso-Brazilian literary collections in the United States.

272.   Fernández, Oscar. *A Preliminary Listing of Foreign Periodical Holdings
        in the United States and Canada Which Give Coverage to Portuguese and
        Brazilian Language and Literature.* See no. 13.

273.   Nelson, Bonnie E. "Spain, Portugal, Latin America and the Caribbean."
        A Guide to Published Library Catalogs. Metuchen: Scarecrow, 1982.
        123–35.
Items 170–92 list catalogs that pertain to the geographical areas indicated.

Specific Libraries and Collections

274.   Catholic University of America. *Oliveira Lima Library.* 2 vols. Boston:
        Hall, 1970.
        Vol. 1 (A–L): iv + 780 pp.; vol. 2 (M–Z and appendixes): iii + 775 pp.
        A catalog of the Oliveira Lima collection. Besides listing books, which are or-
dered alphabetically, it contains sections devoted to Portuguese *folhetos*, Portuguese
journals, Brazilian journals, Spanish American journals, European journals,
manuscripts, and so on.

275.   Hispanic Society of America. *Catalog of the Library.* 10 vols. Boston: Hall,
        1962. First supp. Boston: Hall, 1970.
        A reproduction of the library's main catalog. Includes book holdings published

since 1700; excludes manuscripts, most periodicals, and books published before 1701.

276.   *A Catalogue of the Greenlee Collection. The Newberry Library, Chicago.*
2 vols. Boston: Hall, 1970.
Vol. 1 (A–Lim): vi + 741 pp.; vol. 2 (Lin–Z): 723 pp.
An alphabetical index of the collection's card catalog. The collection is composed primarily of Portuguese historical and literary titles. See also no. 277.

277.   Welsh, Doris Varner. *A Catalog of the William B. Greenlee Collection of Portuguese History and Literature and the Portuguese Materials in the Newberry Library.* Chicago: Newberry Library, 1953. viii + 342 pp.
A classified bibliography. Contains sections on Portuguese literature (83–105) and philology (106–15) and brief sections on Brazilian literature (183–85) and philology (185–86). Includes a supplement and an index. See also no. 276.

278.   Gillett, Theresa, and Helen McIntyre. *Catalog of Luso-Brazilian Material in the University of New Mexico Libraries.* See no. 15.

Germany

279.   Berlin. Ibero-Amerikanisches Institut. *Schlagwortkatalog des Ibero-Amerikanischen Instituts: Preussischer Kulturbesitz in Berlin.* 30 vols. Boston: Hall, 1977.
Vols. 1–19: general section; vols. 19–23: geographical section; vols. 23–24: section of place names; vols. 24–30: biographical section.
Subject headings are in German. Lists of subject headings are provided in English and Spanish. Includes some Portuguese and Brazilian items.

Netherlands

280.   Bibliotheek der Rijksuniversiteit te Utrecht. *Portugal e o Brasil: Catálogo de livros portugueses e brasileiros e publicações estrangeiras sobre Portugal e Brasil.* 3 vols. Utrecht, 1959–66. 403, 326, and 382 pp.
"Editado pela Biblioteca da Universidade de Utrecht em colaboração com o Instituto de Estudos Hispânicos, Portugueses e Ibero-Americanos da Universidade de Utrecht."
Catalogs the Luso-Brazilian collections of the University of Utrecht Library, the Institute of Hispanic, Portuguese, and Iberoamerican Studies of the University of Utrecht, and other institutes of the university.

United Kingdom

281.   Luso-Brazilian Council. London. *Canning House Library: Author Catalogue (A–Z) and Subject Catalogue (A–Z).* Boston: Hall, 1967. vii + 281 + 286 pp.

Alphabetical catalogs (by author and subject) of the collection, consisting of photocopies of the card catalog followed by lists of serial publications belonging to the collection. Not classified or annotated. The first supplement has also been published: Boston: Hall, 1973, vii + 288 pp.

Bibliographies of Bibliographies

282. *Bibliographische Berichte.* Frankfurt: Klostermann 1– (1958–).
A current bibliography of bibliographies. Contains sections on national bibliographies, literature, and other areas of knowledge.

283. Foulché-Delbosc, Raymond, and L. Barrau-Dihigo. *Manuel de l'hispanisant.* 2 vols. New York: Hispanic Soc. of America, 1929. New York: Kraus, 1959.
Vol. 1: "Généralités," "Type-bibliographies," "Biographie et biobibliographies," "Bibliographies monographiques," "Archives, bibliothèques et musées," "Collections dispersées"; xxiii + 533 pp.; vol. 2: Index to collections printed between 1579 and 1923, particularly in history and literature; xi + 447 pp.
Dated but still of great use.

284. Zubatsky, David S. "An Annotated Bibliography of Portuguese Author Bibliographies." *Luso-Brazilian Review* 15.1 (1978): 44–62.
Lists 97 bibliographies of 44 Portuguese writers from various periods. Also includes a brief section containing general bibliographies and biobibliographies.

Brazilian Literature

Current Bibliographies and Periodical Indexes

285.   *Bibliografía de publicaciones japonesas sobre América Latina en 1974–* . Tokyo: Inst. Iberoamericano de la U de Sofia, 1975– .
A classified bibliography of Japanese-language materials on Latin America. Includes published Japanese translations of the works of Latin American authors. Title also in Japanese.

286.   "Bibliografía hispanoamericana." *Revista hispánica moderna* 1–15 (1934–47); "Bibliografía hispánica" 16–22 (1948–56); "Bibliografía hispanoamericana" 23–32 (1956–66); "Bibliografía hispánica" 33–35 (1967–69).
A classified bibliography. Lists books, articles, dissertations, and book reviews. For many years, the most comprehensive of such bibliographies. Sections called "Bibliografía hispanoamericana" include only items pertaining to the literature of Latin America; Peninsular materials are indexed in the bibliographies of the *Revista de filología española* and the *Nueva revista de filología hispánica.*

287.   "Bibliographie." *Revue d'histoire du théâtre.* See no. 147.

288.   *Bibliographie latino-américaine d'articles.* Paris: Inst. des Hautes Etudes de l'Amérique Latine, 1975– .
Semiannual. Includes Brazilian literature.

289.   *Bulletin bibliographique Amérique Latine. Analyse des publications françaises et recherche bibliographique automatisée sur le fichier FRANCIS.* Paris: Editions Recherche sur les Civilisations. 1– (1981–).
A current bibliography of French publications on Latin America. Lists books, articles, dissertations, unpublished reports, and so on. "Analyse des publications françaises" includes a section entitled "Langues et littératures" and several indexes. "Recherche bibliographique automatisée sur le fichier FRANCIS" includes two sections, "Histoire et sciences de la littérature" and "Sciences du langage."

290.   *Bulletin signalétique . . . .* See no. 148.

291.   *Handbook of Latin American Studies.* Vols. 1–13 (1935–47). Cambridge: Harvard UP, 1936–51. Vols. 14–40 (1948–74). Gainesville: U of Florida

P, 1951–78. Vols. 41– (1975–). Austin: U of Texas P, 1979– .
A current bibliography. Long an important reference tool for Latin American literature. Lists materials selected and annotated by a team of scholars in the various fields. Volumes 1–25 include a bibliography of selected literary works and studies in literary history and criticism for each year. As of volume 26, the literature bibliography is published in the humanities volume, which currently alternates with a social sciences volume.

292.   *Hispanic American Periodicals Index, 1970–1974.* 3 vols. Los Angeles: U of California, Latin American Center, 1984; *Hispanic American Periodicals Index.* Los Angeles: U of California, Latin American Center, 1975– .
Lists works appearing in some 200 journals published in Latin America or on Latin American topics.

293.   Columbus Memorial Library. *Index to Latin American Periodical Literature 1929–1960.* 8 vols. Boston: Hall, 1962; suppl. 1961–65. 2 vols. Boston: Hall, 1968; supp. 1966–70. 2 vols. Boston: Hall, 1980.

294.   ———. *Index to Latin American Periodicals: Humanities and Social Sciences.* Vols. 1–2. Boston: Hall, 1961–62; vols. 3–9. Metuchen: Scarecrow, 1963–69.
Nos. 293–94 index several hundred periodicals found in the Columbus Memorial Library. Classified by author and subject.

295.   *MLA Directory of Periodicals.* See no. 21.

296.   *MLA International Bibliography.* See no. 22.

297.   "Notas bibliográficas. . . ." See no. 26.

298.   *Romanische Bibliographie.* See no. 33.

299.   *The Year's Work in Modern Language Studies.* See no. 39.

Library and Resource Guides

300.   Garlant, Julia, Laurence Hallewell, et al. *Latin American Bibliography: A Guide to Sources of Information and Research.* London: U of London, Inst. of Latin American Studies, 1978. xviii + 227 pp.
A sourcebook for Latin American Studies.

301.   Jackson, William Vernon. *Library Guide for Brazilian Studies.* See no. 19.

302.   Lauerhass, Ludwig, Jr. *Library Resources on Latin America: Research Guide and Bibliographic Introduction.* Latin American Collections in the

UCLA Library Guides, ser. A, no. 2. Los Angeles: U of California, Latin American Center and University Library, 1978. vii + 95 pp.
Contents: "Introduction," "General Bibliography and Reference Materials: The Subject Search," "Spanish American and Brazilian Bibliography and Reference Materials: The Author Approach," "Books and Monographs: The Classification Approach," "Periodicals," "International Agency and Government Publications," "Newspapers," "Special Materials," "Research beyond the Base Library," "Index." A general library guide for the Latin Americanist, with emphasis on the UCLA libraries. Prepared by a noted Latin Americanist bibliographer.

General Reference Works
Bibliographies

303. Becco, Horacio Jorge. *Bibliografía general de las artes del espectáculo en la América Latina.* Paris: UNESCO, 1977. 118 pp.
A classified bibliography. Most of the 1,797 items pertain to Latin American theater.

304. *Bibliografía general de la literatura hispanoamericana.* Paris: UNESCO, 1972. 187 pp.
Contains: "Período colonial" (17–63), compiled by Guillermo Lohman Villena and Luis Jaime Cisneros, "Siglo XIX" (67–128), compiled by Julio Ortega, and "Época contemporánea" (129–66), compiled by Horacio Jorge Becco. Each period is subdivided into "Bibliografías generales," "Bibliografías regionales," and "Historias generales."

305. Carpeaux, Otto Maria. *Pequena bibliografia crítica da literatura brasileira.* Rev. ed. Rio de Janeiro: Tecnoprint, 1979. 470 pp.
"Nova edição, com um apêndice de Assis Brasil, incluindo 47 novos autores." A standard reference tool. Partially annotated. Includes more than 3,500 bibliographical entries about the works of major Brazilian authors from the baroque period to the present day. Also lists general bibliographies and literary histories (general, regional, of genres, of periods). Briefly remarks on each period and literary movement and includes minimal biographical and critical data and a list of main works for each author. Onomastic and author indexes. First edition, 1951.

306. Chamberlain, Bobby J. "A Consumer Guide to Developing a Brazilian-Literature Reference Library." *Hispania* 64 (1981): 260–64.
A brief, partially annotated bibliography of the most important (and available) reference works needed for a Brazilian-literature reference collection. The author divides the works listed into 2 categories, "First Priority" and "Second Priority." Includes mostly literary histories and bibliographies, dictionaries of literature, and anthologies.

307. Ford, Jeremiah Denis Matthias, Arthur F. Whitten, and Maxwell I. Raphael. *A Tentative Bibliography of Brazilian Belles-Lettres.* Cambridge: Harvard UP, 1931. vi + 201 pp.

Lists only primary (not secondary) sources: poetry, drama, fiction, and so on. Also includes grammars, dictionaries, and linguistic studies. Dated; there are several gaps and errors.

308.   Foster, David W. "An Annotated Registry of Scholarly Journals in Hispanic Studies." See no. 154.

309.   Harmon, Ronald M., and Bobby J. Chamberlain. *Brazil: A Working Bibliography in Literature, Linguistics, Humanities and the Social Sciences.* See no. 17.

310.   Lombardi, Mary. *Brazilian Serial Documents: A Selective and Annotated Guide.* Bloomington: Indiana UP, 1974. xxxvii + 445 pp.
Among the documents issued by the Ministério da Educação e Cultura are those of the Conselho Nacional de Cultura, the Biblioteca Nacional, the Instituto Nacional do Livro, and the Fundação Casa de Rui Barbosa.

311.   Lyon, Ted. "Recent (1966-1978) Scholarly Journals Relating to Latin American Literature." *Hispania* 62 (1979): 693-95.
Supplements Foster's "An Annotated Registry of Scholarly Journals in Hispanic Studies" (no. 154).

312.   Maison des Sciences de l'Homme. *Liste mondiale des périodiques spécialisés: Amérique Latine. World List of Specialized Periodicals: Latin America.* Paris: Mouton, 1974. 186 pp.
A classified, descriptive bibliography of 381 periodicals that deal with Latin America. Arranged by country of publication. Includes a subject index. Trilingual (French, English, and Spanish).

313.   Moisés, Massaud, Walter Rela, Bobby J. Chamberlain, and Terry L. Palls. "Selected Bibliography of Brazilian Literature." *Chasqui* 15.2-3 (1986): 49-76.
Classified. Lists 491 book-length items published between 1960 and 1983 relating to Brazilian literature: bibliographies; dictionaries; essays, histories, and criticism; anthologies; and miscellaneous works.

314.   Moraes, Rubens Borba de, and William Berrien. *Manual bibliográfico de estudos brasileiros.* See no. 23.

315.   Moser, Gerald M. "Histories of Brazilian Literature: A Critical Survey." *Revista interamericana de bibliografía* 10 (1960): 117-46.
An annotated bibliography. Contents: "Introduction" "Works in English," "Older Basic Works, Mainly in Portuguese," "Recent Works in Portuguese (1945-1958)." Includes an alphabetical index of authors, compilers, and editors.

316.   Nunes, Maria Luisa. "Resources for the Study of Brazilian Literature." *Neohelicon* 4.1-2 (1976): 225-38.
Contents: "I. General Background," "1. Bibliographies," "2. General Histories of Literature," "3. Literary Genres," "4. Criticism, a Selective Bibliography,"

"5. Newspapers and Reviews," "6. Libraries," "II. Machado de Assis," "1. Complete Works," "2. Bibliography of Critical Works on Machado de Assis," "III. Afro-Brazilian Culture and Brazilian Literature," "1. Afro-Brazilian Bibliography."

A bibliographv of titles recommended for the study of Brazilian literature (and for research on Machado de Assis and on Afro-Brazilian culture).

317.   *Periódicos brasileiros de cultura.* Rio de Janeiro: Inst. Brasileiro de Bibliografia e Documentação, 1968. 280 pp.
A classified bibliography of Brazilian cultural journals. Includes subject and title indexes.

318.   Reis, Antônio Simões dos. *Bibliografia brasileira.* Rio de Janeiro: Simões, 1966.
Vol. 1: 420 pp.
The compiler is again taking up the task begun in 1942–43 (with his *Bibliografia nacional,* no. 319) of producing a current bibliography of Brazilian literature.

319.   ———. *Bibliografia nacional.* 16 fasc. Rio de Janeiro: Valverde, 1942–43.
A classified, current bibliography of Brazilian books.

320.   Sable, Martin H. *A Guide to Latin American Studies.* 2 vols. Los Angeles: U of California, Latin American Center, 1967.
Vol. 1: lxxv + 373 pp.; vol. 2: lxxvi–lxxxi + 374–783.
A classified, annotated bibliography. Seems to prefer English translations to the Portuguese and Spanish originals. Items 2881–3112 pertain to literature.

321.   Sánchez, Luis Alberto. *Repertorio bibliográfico de la literatura latinoamericana.* Ser. A. 5 vols. Santiago: U de Chile; Lima: U Nacional Mayor de San Marcos, 1955–69.
A bibliography with brief annotations. Contains 6,449 entries. Volume 2 includes materials pertinent to Brazil.

322.   Sodré, Nelson Werneck. *O que se deve ler para conhecer o Brasil.* See no. 36.

323.   Sousa, José Galante de. "Bibliografia." *Introdução ao estudo da literatura brasileira.* Rio de Janeiro: Inst. Nacional do Livro, Ministério da Educação e Cultura, 1963. 73–241.
Contents: "Biobibliografias," "Bibliografias," "Catálogos," "Obras gerais—sínteses," "Épocas," "Gêneros," "Influências—literatura comparada," "Problemas de autoria," "Literatura regional," "Ensaios diversos," "Antologias," "Vária."
Includes only general sources; excludes works about single authors.

324.   ———. *Índice de biobibliografia brasileira.* Rio de Janeiro: Inst. Nacional do Livro, Ministério da Educação e Cultura, 1963. 440 pp.
An alphabetical index of the authors listed in 29 Brazilian biobibliographical works. (Most traditional Brazilian biobibliographies are arranged by the authors' first names.)

325.   Topete, José Manuel. *A Working Bibliography of Brazilian Literature.*
Gainesville: U of Florida P, 1957. xii + 114 pp.
Contents: "Works of General Reference," "Criticism, Essay, Journalism, and
Biography," "The Novel and Other Prose Fiction," "Poetry," "The Theater,"
"Selected English and Spanish Translations."
Annotated. Lists 1,300 items. Index of authors.

326.   Valis, Noël. "Directory of Publication Sources in the Fields of Hispanic
Language and Literature." See no. 37.

327.   Wilgus, A. Curtis. *Latin America, Spain and Portugal: A Selected and
Annotated Bibliographical Guide to Books Published in the United
States.* See no. 158.

328.   Zubatsky, David S. "A Bibliography of Cumulative Indexes to Luso-
Brazilian Journals of the Nineteenth and Twentieth Centuries: Humanities and Social Sciences." See no. 40.

329.   ———. "An International Bibliography of Cumulative Indexes to Journals Publishing Articles on Hispanic Languages and Literatures." See no.
42.

330.   ———. "An International Bibliography of Cumulative Indices to Journals Publishing Articles on Hispanic Languages and Literatures: First
Supplement." See no. 43.

Dictionaries of Literary Terms

331.   Campos, Geir. *Pequeno dicionário de arte poética.* Rio de Janeiro: Tecnoprint, 1965. 220 pp.
First edition, 1960. A brief but useful dictionary of literary terms and poetic
forms, written by a Brazilian poet. Contains 618 entries. Bibliography.

332.   Moisés, Massaud. *Dicionário de termos literários.* 4th ed. São Paulo: Cultrix, 1985. 520 pp.
Contains over 700 entries (literary genres and forms; concepts of literary theory and criticism; rhetorical and poetical terms; literary, artistic, and philosophical
movements; and so on). Perhaps the best Portuguese-language dictionary of literary terms. Still, it lacks most terminology associated with contemporary literary
theory. First edition, 1974.

Dictionaries of Authors and Biobibliographies

333.   Brasil, Assis. *Dicionário prático de literatura brasileira.* Rio de Janeiro:
Tecnoprint, 1979. 324 pp.
A biobibliography of Brazilian authors.

334. Brinches, Victor. *Dicionário biobibliográfico luso-brasileiro.* See no. 162.

335. *The Cambridge Encyclopedia of Latin America and the Caribbean.* Ed.
Simon Collier, Harold Blakemore, and Thomas E. Skidmore. Cambridge:
Cambridge UP, 1985. 456 pp.
Includes articles on Brazilian literature (369–72) and Brazilian Portuguese
(348–50).

336. Coelho, Jacinto do Prado. *Dicionário de literatura: Literatura portuguesa,
literatura brasileira, literatura galega, estilística literária.* See no. 165.

337. *Diccionario de autores iberoamericanos.* See no. 166.

338. *Dictionary of Brazilian Literature.* Ed. Irwin Stern. New York: Green-
wood, l + 402 pp. 1988.
Includes more than 200 entries on writers, movements, and other literary topics.
Covers the entire history of Brazilian literature, giving special attention to
twentieth-century writers. Each entry indicates the author's major works and lists
several recent critical studies. Prepared by a team of critics. Includes a chronology, an introduction, and an index. Extremely useful.

339. *Encyclopedia of World Literature in the Twentieth Century.* See no. 167.

340. Foster, David William, and Roberto Reis. *A Dictionary of Contemporary
Brazilian Authors.* Tempe: Arizona State U, Center for Latin American
Studies, 1981. 152 pp.
A critical dictionary of living and recently deceased Brazilian authors. Empha-
sizes new writers. Compiled by a team of 35 contributors, which helps to explain
a certain lack of uniformity of article length and style. Very useful.

341. *Latin American Literature in the Twentieth Century: A Guide.* Ed.
Leonard S. Klein. New York: Ungar, 1986. x + 278 pp.
Based on the *Encyclopedia of World Literature in the Twentieth Century* (no.
167). Includes dictionary entries on Brazilian literature (47–55) and on 17 individual Brazilian authors (55–92). Index of articles on Brazilian authors.

342. *Latin American Writers.* Ed. Carlos A. Solé and Maria Isabel Abreu. 3
vols. New York: Scribner's, in press.
Contains articles on some 25 Brazilian writers from the colonial period to the
present day. Includes a bibliography of principal works and a listing of biographical and critical studies for each author. Supplementary volumes are planned.

343. Lincoln, Joseph Newhall. *Charts of Brazilian Literature.* Ann Arbor: n.p.,
1947. 86 pp.
Provides biobibliographical information on Brazilian authors.

344. Luft, Celso Pedro. *Dicionário de literatura portuguesa e brasileira.* See
no. 168.

60   *General Reference Works*

345.   Menezes, Raimundo de. *Dicionário literário brasileiro.* 2nd ed, rev. and
       enl. Rio de Janeiro: LTC, 1978. xix + 803 pp.
       A biobibliographical dictionary. Includes biographical, critical, and bib-
       liographical data on 3,800 Brazilian authors. Also contains an index of Brazil-
       ian literary pseudonyms, a section with brief articles on "ismos literários, escolas
       e academias," and a general bibliography. First edition, 5 vols., 1969. An extremely
       useful work, now published in a single volume.

346.   Ocampo de Gómez, Aurora M. *Novelistas iberoamericanos contem-
       poráneos: Obra y bibliografía crítica.* . . . Cuadernos del Centro de Es-
       tudios Literarios 2, 4, 6, 10, 11. México: UNAM, 1971–81.
       A biobibliography of major contemporary Latin American authors. Includes
       both primary and secondary sources.

347.   *Pequeno dicionário de literatura brasileira.* Ed. José Paulo Paes and Mas-
       saud Moisés. 2nd ed., rev. and enl. São Paulo: Cultrix, 1980. 462 pp.
       A biobibliographical dictionary. First edition, 1967. Second printing, corrected,
       1969. Includes "mais de 350 autores, dos primórdios do século XVI aos dias de
       hoje, estudados em verbetes individuais, que fornecem, de cada autor, dados bi-
       ográficos sumários, apreciação crítica da obra, relação dos livros principais e rol
       de fontes críticas para seu estudo." Also contains entries on prominent literary
       works, literary movements and periods, genres, poetic forms, and so on. The prod-
       uct of a team of 31 literary critics. Each article bears the initials of its author. Ex-
       tremely useful.

348.   Sacramento Blake, Augusto Victorino Alves. *Diccionario bibliographico
       brazileiro.* 7 vols. Nendeln, Liechtenstein: Kraus, 1969.
       Vol. 1 (A–Br): 1883, xxiv + 440 pp.; vol. 2 (C–Fr): 1893, viii + 479 pp.; vol.
       3 (Fr–Jo): 1985, vi + 520 pp.; vol. 4 (Jo): 1898, 529 pp.; vol. 5 (Jo–Ly): 1899, 495
       pp.; vol. 6 (M–Pe): 1900, 405 pp.; vol. 7 (Pe–Zo): 1902, 440 pp. + *Indice al-
       phabetico* (vi + 127 pp.).
       A facsimile reprint of the original edition (1883–1902). Each volume has an ap-
       pendix. Arranged by authors' first names. The index, prepared by Jango Fischer
       and published originally in a separate volume in 1937 (Rio de Janeiro: Nacional),
       is arranged by authors' surnames. Another Brazilian edition was published in 7
       volumes by the Conselho Federal de Cultura (1970). See also Alexandre Eulálio,
       "Índice do *Dicionario bibliographico brazileiro* de A. V. A. Sacramento Blake,"
       Revista do livro [Rio de Janeiro] 5 (1957): 213–36; 6 (1957): 219–32; 7 (1957):
       225–42; 8 (1957): 265–84.

349.   Seymour-Smith, Martin. *The New Guide to Modern World Literature.*
       See no. 172.

350.   Silva, Inocêncio Francisco da. *Dicionario bibliographico portuguez.* See
       no. 173.

351.   Velho Sobrinho, J. F. *Dicionário biobibliográfico brasileiro.* 2 vols. Rio
       de Janeiro: Pongetti, 1937–40.
       Vol. 1: 704 pp.; vol. 2: 615 pp.

Covers only the letters A and B. See also Célio Assis do Carmo, "Índice do *Dicionário biobibliográfico* de J. F. Velho Sobrinho," *Revista do livro* [Rio de Janeiro] 12 (1958): 253–69; 13 (1959): 261–73; 14 (1959): 197–211.

Genres

Popular Poetry

352. Almeida, Átila Augusto F. de, and José Alves Sobrinho. *Dicionário biobibliográfico de repentistas e poetas de bancada.* 2 vols. Jõao Pessoa: Editora Universitária; Campina Grande: Centro de Ciências e Tecnologia, 1978.
Vol. 1 (1–320): "Apresentação" (9–52); an alphabetical listing of "todos os nomes de cantadores e poetas populares" of the *literatura de cordel* (popular chapbook poetry) of northeastern Brazil; also includes biographical and bibliographical data and the acrostics used by many of the poets. Vol. 2 (321–672): An alphabetical list of *folheto* titles, indicating their authors.

353. Casa de Rui Barbosa. *Literatura popular em verso: Catálogo, Tomo I.* Rio de Janeiro: Ministério da Educação e Cultura; Casa de Rui Barbosa, 1961. xvi + 399 pp.
A descriptive catalog of 1,000 *folhetos de cordel* published in Brazil. Includes indexes of authors, titles of poems, first lines, and subjects.

354. Curran, Mark Joseph. *Selected Bibliography of History and Politics in Brazilian Popular Poetry.* Tempe: Arizona State U, Center for Latin American Studies, 1971. 26 pp.
Pertains to *literatura de cordel.*

355. Luyten, Joseph Maria. *Bibliografia especializada sobre literatura popular em verso.* São Paulo: Escola de Comunicações e Artes da U de São Paulo, 1981. 104 pp.

Poetry

356. Reis, Antônio Simões dos. *Poetas do Brasil: Bibliografia.* 2 vols. Rio de Janeiro: Simões, 1949–51.
Vol. 1 (A–Andrade): 176 pp.; vol. 2 (Andrade–Azul): 177–303.
A biobibliography of Brazilian poets. Includes critical comments. Author and title indexes.

Theater

357. *Bibliografia de dramaturgia brasileira.* São Paulo: Escola de Comunicações e Artes da U de São Paulo; Associação Museu Lasar Segall, 1981– .
Vol. 1: A–M.

A listing of plays, arranged by playwright. Followed by title and character indexes.

358.   Hoffman, Herbert H. *Latin American Play Index, Vol. 1: 1920–1963.* Metuchen: Scarecrow, 1984. v + 147 pp.

359.   ———. *Latin American Play Index, Vol. 2: 1962–1980.* Metuchen: Scarecrow, 1983. iv + 131 pp.

A 2-volume index of plays (nos. 358–59) written by Spanish American and Brazilian playwrights. Indicates the anthologies and journals where such works were published and the issues of the *Handbook of Latin American Studies* (no. 291) where they are reviewed. Author and title indexes.

360.   Lyday, Leon F., and George Woodyard. *A Bibliography of Latin American Theater Criticism, 1940–1974.* Guides and Bibliographic Series 10. Austin: U of Texas, Inst. of Latin American Studies, 1976. xvii + 243 pp. Partially annotated. Contains 2,360 items. A revision and enlargement of the authors' "Studies on the Latin American Theatre, 1960–1969," *Theatre Documentation* 2 (Fall 1969–Spring 1970): 49–84, which lists 694 items. See also Charles A. Carpenter, "Latin American Theater Criticism, 1966–1974: Some Addenda to Lyday and Woodyard," *Revista interamericana de bibliografía* 30.3 (1980): 246–53.

361.   Rela, Walter. "Contribución a la bibliografía del teatro brasileño." *Cebela* 1 (1965): 109–29.
A listing of individual playwrights' works along with a bibliography of theater criticism.

362.   Universidade de São Paulo, Departamento de Biblioteconomia e Documentação. *Bibliografia sobre teatro paulista.* São Paulo: Escola de Comunicações e Artes, Departamento de Jornalismo e Editoração, U de São Paulo, 1972. 103 pp.
Contents: "Obras," "Revistas," "Jornais," "Bienais de Teatro" "Índice."
A classified, annotated bibliography of the theater of São Paulo state.

363.   Sousa, José Galante de. *O teatro no Brasil, II: Subsídios para uma bio-bibliografia do teatro no Brasil.* Rio de Janeiro: Ministério da Educação e Cultura, Inst. Nacional do Livro, 1960. 581 pp.
A biobibliographical dictionary of Brazilian playwrights from the colonial period to 1960. Volume 1 is a history of the national theater.

Short Story and Novella

364.   Carmo, Pinto do. *Novelas e novelistas brasileiros: Indicações bibliográficas.* Rio de Janeiro: Simões, 1957. 67 pp.
Annotated. A bibliography of the Brazilian novella.

365. Gomes, Celeuta Moreira. *O conto brasileiro e sua crítica: Bibliografia (1841-1974).* 2 vols. Rio de Janeiro: Biblioteca Nacional, 1977. Vol. 1 (A-L): xxi + 285 pp.; vol. 2 (M-Z): 287-654. Annotated. Index. Also includes a bibliographical supplement on short-story anthologies. Critical studies of short stories or specific authors are listed immediately after the authors' bibliographies. An expanded version of Gomes and Aguiar's 1968 bibliography of the Brazilian short story (no. 366).

366. Gomes, Celeuta Moreira, and Thereza da Silva Aguiar. *Bibliografia do conto brasileiro: 1841-1967.* 2 vols. Rio de Janeiro: Biblioteca Nacional, 1968. A bibliography arranged by author's name. Volume 87 of the *Anais da Biblioteca Nacional.* See also no. 365.

Novel

367. Grupo Gente Nova. *Dicionário crítico do moderno romance brasileiro: 1-2 (A-V).* Ed. Pedro Américo Maia. Belo Horizonte: Grupo Gente Nova, 1970. 487 pp. Used a team of 13 contributors. Includes original critical commentary (often extensive) and excerpts from previously published critical studies on the works of fiction of more than 300 modern Brazilian authors. Does not include biographical data. The 2 parts were also published separately.

368. ———. *Dicionário crítico do moderno romance brasileiro. Suplemento 1: Brasil—Ficção 70.* Belo Horizonte, 1971? 71 pp. Contents: "Brasil, ficção 70," "A crítica da ficção." Provides critical commentary on the Brazilian fiction of 1970 and on several studies of literary criticism published in 1970-71.

369. Rio de Janeiro. Biblioteca Nacional. *O romance brasileiro: Catálogo da exposição.* Rio de Janeiro: Biblioteca Nacional, 1974. 86 pp. Contents: "Precursores e Romantismo," "Naturalismo—Realismo—Simbolismo," "Do Modernismo à atualidade." Includes bibliographical information.

Folk Narrative

370. MacGregor-Villarreal, Mary. "Brazilian Folk-Narrative Scholarship: A Critical Survey and Selective Annotated Bibliography." Diss. U of California, Los Angeles. 1981. 260 pp.

Children's Literature

371. *Bibliografia brasileira de livros infantis.* Rio de Janeiro: Sindicato Nacional dos Escritores de Livros, 1967- . A current bibliography. Annual.

372.   Coelho, Nelly Novaes. *Dicionário crítico da literatura infantil brasileira.*
       São Paulo: Quíron, 1983. 963 pp.
    A critical dictionary of Brazilian authors of children's literature, covering
1882-1982.

373.   Fundação Nacional do Livro Infantil e Juvenil. *Bibliografia analítica da
       literatura infantil e juvenil publicada no Brasil (1965-1974).* São Paulo:
       Melhoramentos; Brasília: Inst. Nacional do Livro, 1977. 384 pp.
    "Trabalho realizado sob o patrocínio do Instituto Nacional de Estudos e
Pesquisas Educacionais (INEP)."
    An extensive classified, annotated bibliography. Includes indexes as well as list-
ings of critical studies on children's and young people's literature.

374.   São Paulo. Brasil. Departamento de Bibliotecas Infanto-Juvenis. *Bib-
       liografia de literatura infantil em língua portuguesa.* São Paulo, 1953.
    Second edition, enl., 1955, 280 pp. The first supplement covers 1955-57; the
second, 1958-62 (1964; 60 pp.); third, 1962-68 (1969; 92 pp.); fourth, 1968-70
(1972; 102 pp.); fifth, 1970-73; sixth, 1973-76 (1977; 71 pp.).

States

Maranhão

375.   Moraes, Jomar. *Bibliografia crítica da literatura maranhense.* São Luís:
       Dept. de Cultura do Maranhão, 1972. 122 pp.
    A critical, annotated bibliography of *maranhense* authors from the colonial
period to the twentieth century.

Rio de Janeiro

376.   Ribeiro Filho, João de Souza. *Dicionário bibliográfico de escritores ca-
       riocas (1565-1965).* Rio de Janeiro: Brasiliana, 1965. 285 pp.
    A biobibliography of carioca authors and of writers who have written about
the city of Rio. Published at the time of the city's quadricentennial.

Rio Grande do Sul

377.   Martins, Ari. *Escritores do Rio Grande do Sul.* Porto Alegre: U Federal
       do Rio Grande do Sul, Inst. Estadual do Livro, 1978. 636 pp.
    A biobibliographical dictionary of the authors of Rio Grande do Sul.

378.   Villas-Boas, Pedro. *Notas de bibliografia sul-rio-grandense: Autores.*
       Porto Alegre: Nação; Brasília: Inst. Nacional do Livro, 1974. 615 pp.
    A biobibliographical dictionary of the authors of Rio Grande do Sul. Includes
an index of abbreviations and pseudonyms used and an index of authors listed.

São Paulo

379.   Melo, Luís Correa de. *Dicionário de autores paulistas.* São Paulo: Andrioli, 1954. 678 pp.
Includes biographical and bibliographical data for each author.

Special Topics and Miscellaneous
Criticism

380.   Foster, David W., and Virginia Ramos Foster. *Modern Latin American Literature.* 2 vols. New York: Ungar, 1975.
Contains selected critical commentary from scholars around the world on the works of 183 modern Latin American authors, with "particular stress on their reception in the United States" (1: v). All articles have been translated into English.

Afro-Brazilians

381.   Alves, Henrique L. *Bibliografia afro-brasileira: Estudos sobre o negro.* 2nd ed., rev. and enl. Rio de Janeiro: Cátedra, 1979. 181 pp.
Includes literature items. Arranged by author or, if anonymous, by title.

382.   Porter, Dorothy B. *Afro-Braziliana: A Working Bibliography.* See no. 28.

Women

383.   Bittencourt, Adalzira. *Dicionário bio-bibliográfico de mulheres ilustres, notáveis e intelectuais do Brasil.* 3 vols. Rio de Janeiro: Pongetti, 1969–72. Vol. 1 (A–Alz): 190 pp.; vol. 2 (Am–Anz): 191–419; vol. 3 (Ao–By): 421–676. Illustrated.

Reference Works Dealing with Particular Periods, Authors, or Works
Colonial Period
General

384.   "Literature of the Renaissance." *Studies in Philology.* See no. 194.

385.   Moraes, Rubens Borba de. *Bibliografia brasileira do período colonial.* São Paulo: Inst. de Estudos Brasileiros, 1969. xxii + 437 pp.

"Catálogo comentado das obras dos autores nascidos no Brasil e publicados antes de 1808." An annotated, illustrated bibliography.

386. ———. *Bibliographia Brasiliana.* Rev. and enl. ed. 2 vols. Los Angeles: U of California, Latin American Center; Rio de Janeiro: Kosmos, 1983. Vol. 1 (A-L): 502 pp.; vol. 2 (M-Z): 503-1074.
First edition, 1958 (Amsterdam and Rio de Janeiro: Colibris). An annotated bibliography of rare books on Brazil published between 1504 and 1900 and of books written by Brazilian authors during the colonial period.

Authors

Padre Antônio Vieira

387. Leite, Serafim. *História da Companhia de Jesus no Brasil. Tomo IX, escritores: De N a Z (suplemento biobibliográfico II).* Rio de Janeiro: Inst. Nacional do Livro, 1949. 192-363.
Contents: "Sermões," "Cartas," "Obras várias," "Traduções," "Inéditos," "Biografias e outros escritos a Vieira ou sobre Vieira."
An annotated bibliography of the works of Padre Antônio Vieira (1608-97). Lists primary and secondary sources.

Nineteenth and Early Twentieth Centuries

General

388. Elkins, A. C., Jr., and L. S. Forstner, eds. *The Romantic Movement Bibliography, 1936-1970.* . . . See no. 203.

Authors

Manuel Antônio de Almeida

389. Rebelo, Marques [Eddy Dias da Cruz]. *Bibliografia de Manuel Antônio de Almeida.* Rio de Janeiro: Ministério da Educação e Saúde, Inst. Nacional do Livro, 1951. 188 pp.
A bibliography of primary and secondary sources. Lists 258 items. Partially annotated. Includes an index and some engravings.

José de Alencar

390. Leão, Múcio. *José de Alencar: Ensaio biobibliográfico.* Rio de Janeiro: Academia Brasileira de Letras, 1955. 73 pp.
Includes sections entitled "Tentativa de Bibliografia de José de Alencar" and "Algumas fontes sobre José de Alencar."

391. Rio de Janeiro. Biblioteca Nacional. *José de Alencar: Catálogo da exposição*. Rio de Janeiro: Biblioteca Nacional, 1977. 91 pp.
   Contents: "Manuscritos," "Obras," "Teatro," "Músicas inspiradas em obras de Alencar," "Ilustrações."

Antônio de Castro Alves

392. Horch, Hans Jürgen W. *Bibliografia de Castro Alves*. Rio de Janeiro: Ministério da Educação e Cultura, Inst. Nacional do Livro, 1960. 259 pp.
   Contents: "Manuscritos e fac-símiles," "Obra poética," "Traduções," "Poesias musicadas," "Poesias perdidas," "Trabalhos em prosa," "Correspondência," "Edições," "Índice das poesias e obras do poeta," "Índice onomástico," "Índice das publicações periódicas."
   An annotated, classified bibliography of the works of Antônio de Castro Alves.

393. Rio de Janeiro. Biblioteca Nacional. *Castro Alves: Catálogo da exposição*. Rio de Janeiro: Biblioteca Nacional, Div. de Publicações e Divulgação, 1971. 68 pp.
   Contents: "Obras de Castro Alves," "Influências literárias," "Documentário," "Bibliografia," "Retratos de Castro Alves," "Outros retratos," "Ilustrações."

João Ribeiro

394. Leão, Múcio. *João Ribeiro: Ensaio biobibliográfico*. Rio de Janeiro: Academia Brasileira de Letras, 1964. 89 pp.
   Includes sections entitled "Bibliografia," "Plano das obras de João Ribeiro," "Algumas fontes sobre João Ribeiro."

395. Reis, Antônio Simões dos. *João Ribeiro: Bibliografia sobre a sua obra*. Rio de Janeiro: Ministério da Educação e Cultura, Inst. Nacional do Livro, 1960. 45 pp.
   Organized by year.

Joaquim Maria Machado de Assis

396. Sousa, José Galante de. *Bibliografia de Machado de Assis*. Rio de Janeiro: Inst. Nacional do Livro, 1955. 772 pp.
   The most complete bibliography of the writer's works. The first part includes "os pseudônimos e os trabalhos anônimos, as várias edições das obras aparecidas em livro, as versões, a colaboração em periódicos e em obras diversas, as transcrições, os prefácios, manuscritos, fac-símiles, etc." (87). The second part is a chronological index of the author's works.

397. ———. *Fontes para o estudo de Machado de Assis*. 2nd ed., rev. Rio de Janeiro: Inst. Nacional do Livro, 1969. 326 pp.

First edition, 1958. Lists, in chronological order (1857–1957), critical studies of Machado's works; indicates the content of each study. The second edition also includes a supplement of critical studies published between 1958 and 1968. An important reference tool.

398.   Massa, Jean-Michel. *Bibliographie descriptive, analytique et critique de Machado de Assis.* Rio de Janeiro: São José, 1965. 225 pp.
A bibliography of critical studies published in 1957 and 1958. Lists 713 items.

399.   Bagby Júnior, Alberto I. "Eighteen Years of Machado de Assis: A Critical Annotated Bibliography for 1956–74." *Hispania* 58 (1975): 648–83.
A critically annotated bibliography. The compiler regards it as a continuation and updating of the bibliographies of Sousa and Massa (nos. 396–98). Divided into 2 main sections, "Works by Assis" and "Works about Assis." Includes an addendum for 1972–74.

400.   Pati, Francisco. *Dicionário de Machado de Assis: História e biografia das personagens.* 2nd ed. São Paulo: Conselho Estadual de Cultura, 1972. 343 pp.
"Nova redação." Essentially identical to the first edition (São Paulo: Rede Latina, 1958). Divided into 2 parts, "Contos" and "Romances."

Euclides da Cunha

401.   Reis, Irene Monteiro. *Bibliografia de Euclides da Cunha.* Rio de Janeiro: Ministério da Educação e Cultura, Inst. Nacional do Livro, 1971. 422 pp.
Contents: "Cronologia de Euclides," "Obras de Euclides da Cunha," "Correspondência impressa," "Manuscritos," "Índice."
Lists 3,010 items.

402.   Venâncio Filho, Francisco. *Euclides da Cunha.* Rio de Janeiro: Conselho Nacional de Geografia, IBGE, 1949. 37 pp.
Contents: "Bibliografia de Euclides da Cunha," "Bibliografia sobre Euclides da Cunha." The second section contains 350 titles.

Leandro Gomes de Barros

403.   Batista, Sebastião Nunes Hugolino de Sena. *Bibliografia prévia de Leandro Gomes de Barros.* Rio de Janeiro: Biblioteca Nacional, 1971. 97 pp.
A bibliography of the popular verse of this early master of *literatura de cordel.*

Henrique Coelho Neto

404.   Coelho Neto, Paulo. *Bibliografia de Coelho Neto.* Rio de Janeiro: Inst. Nacional do Livro, 1972. 326 pp.
Contents: "I. Pseudônimos," "II. Cronologia," "III. Bibliografia," "A. Obra

seleta," "B. Obras escolhidas," "C. Contribuição em obras de outros autores," "D. Literatura brasileira," "E. Obras individuais do autor," "F. Traduções," "G. Trabalhos esparsos (em capítulos de livros, revistas e jornais)," "H. Trabalhos esparsos (em manuscrito)," "IV. Fontes de informação," "A. Estudos biobibliográficos (em livros, capítulos de livros, separatas, revistas ou jornais)," "B. Documentos iconográficos," "V. Notas finais do autor," "VI. Índices."
A partially annotated bibliography. Lists 2,966 items. A shorter edition appeared in 1956.

Afonso Henriques de Lima Barreto

405. Nunes, Maria Luisa. *Lima Barreto: Bibliography and Translations*. Boston: Hall, 1979. 227 pp.
A bibliography of the author's works and of critical studies written about them, followed by English translations of *Vida e morte de M. J. Gonzaga de Sá* and *Clara dos Anjos*.

Modernism

General

406. Placer, Xavier. *Modernismo brasileiro: Bibliografia, 1918-1971*. Rio de Janeiro: Biblioteca Nacional, 1972. 401 pp.
Contents: "1. Bibliografia," "1.1. Livros e folhetos (bibliografia, filologia, artes, Brasil)," "1.2. Periódicos," "1.2.1. Modernistas e outros," "1.3. Artigos de periódicos," "1.3.1. Revistas," "1.3.2. Jornais," "2. Siglas e abreviaturas," "3. Títulos dos periódicos," "4. Índice."
A classified, annotated bibliography.

Authors

Mário de Andrade

407. Rio de Janeiro. Biblioteca Nacional. *Exposição Mário de Andrade*. Rio de Janeiro: Ministério da Educação e Cultura, Biblioteca Nacional, Div. de Publicações e Divulgação, 1970. 73 pp.
A catalog of the exposition. Contents: "Obras de Mário de Andrade," "Antologias," "Documentário," "Poemas dedicados a Mário de Andrade," "Bibliografia," "Caricaturas," "Fotografias."

Graciliano Ramos

408. Cunha, Antônio. "Graciliano Ramos: An Annotated Bibliography." MA thesis. San Diego State Coll., 1970.
A bibliography of primary and secondary sources. Annotated and classified.

409.   Rio de Janeiro. Biblioteca Nacional. *Exposição Graciliano Ramos, 1892-1953.* Rio de Janeiro: Biblioteca Nacional, 1963. 24 pp.
Includes works both by and about the author.

410.   Sant'Ana, Moacir Medeiros de. *Graciliano Ramos: Achegas bibliográficas.* Maceió: Arquivo Público de Alagoas, 1973. 94 pp.

José Lins do Rego

411.   Rio de Janeiro. Biblioteca Nacional. Seção de Promoções Culturais. *José Lins do Rego, 1901-1957: Catálogo da exposição.* Rio de Janeiro: Biblioteca Nacional, 1981. 95 pp.
Lists works both by and about the author.

Carlos Drummond de Andrade

412.   Py, Fernando. *Bibliografia comentada de Carlos Drummond de Andrade, 1918-1930.* Rio de Janeiro: Olympio; Fundação Casa de Rui Barbosa; Brasília: Inst. Nacional do Livro, 1980. ix + 176 pp.
"Em convênio com o Instituto Nacional do Livro e com a colaboração da Fundação Casa Rui Barbosa, Ministério da Educação e Cultura, Brasília."
Divided into "Índice cronológico," "Pseudônimos e afins," "Edição," "Índice geral de títulos," "Índice onomástico geral."
A bibliography of Drummond de Andrade's early works.

Jorge Amado

413.   Almeida, Alfredo Wagner Berno de. "Anexo: Uma bibliografia de Jorge Amado." *Jorge Amado: Política e literatura. Um estudo sobre a trajetória intelectual de Jorge Amado.* Rio de Janeiro: Campus, 1979. 275-313.
Contents: "1. As fontes," "2. Bibliografia," "2.1. A produção intelectual do autor," "2.2. Entrevistas, depoimentos, inquéritos e declarações," "2.3. A produção intelectual sobre Jorge Amado e sua obra."
Includes in the bibliography of primary sources many articles, reviews, prefaces, and excerpts heretofore not listed, and in the bibliography of secondary sources numerous critical essays previously unreported. There are gaps.

414.   Tavares, Paulo. "Bibliografias." *O baiano Jorge Amado e sua obra.* Rio de Janeiro: Record, 1980. 53-139.
The third part of Tavares' book. Contents: "I. Bibliografia de Jorge Amado," "1. Obras publicadas," "2. Co-autorias," "3. Adaptações," "II. Bibliografia sobre Jorge Amado."
Includes in the secondary sources section books, selected articles, and PhD dissertations. A selective study.

415.   ———. *Criaturas de Jorge Amado.* 2nd ed., enl. Rio de Janeiro: Record; Brasília: Inst. Nacional do Livro, 1985. xx + 514 pp.

"Dicionário biográfico de todas as personagens imaginárias, seguido de índice onomástico das personalidades reais ou lendárias mencionadas, de elenco dos animais e aves com nomes próprios e de roteiro toponímico da obra de ficção de Jorge Amado, totalizando 4.910 verbetes." Includes the characters of *Farda fardão camisola de dormir* (i.e., up to 1979). First edition, São Paulo: Martins, 1969; includes characters of *Dona Flor e seus dois maridos* (i.e., up to 1966).

416.   *Zhorzhy Amadu: Biobibliograficheskiy ukazatiel.* Moskva: Kniga, 1965. 47 pp.
Lists primary sources as well as books and articles about them written in Portuguese and English. Also lists Russian translations of Amado's works and essays published in the Soviet Union about those works. Introductory study and many bibliographical items in Russian. Above title transliterated from the Cyrillic alphabet.

João Guimarães Rosa

417.   Doyle, Plínio. "Contribuição à bibliografia de e sobre João Guimarães Rosa." *Em memória de João Guimarães Rosa.* Rio de Janeiro: Olympio, 1968. 193–255.
Contents: "I. Bibliografia de João Guimarães Rosa," "A. Livros," "B. Prefácios," "C. Discursos," "D. Correspondência publicada," "E. Traduções [those written by Rosa]," "F. Trabalhos em publicações brasileiras," "G. Obras de João Guimarães Rosa adaptadas para teatro, cinema e literatura infantil," "H. Trabalhos incluídos em antologias nacionais e estrangeiras," "I. Traduções [of Rosa's works]," "II. Bibliografia sobre João Guimarães Rosa," "A. Em jornais e periódicos brasileiros," "B. Em jornais e periódicos estrangeiros."
A classified bibliography of almost 900 items. The most complete bibliography of Rosa to date. Needs to be updated; numerous books and critical essays on Rosa have been published since 1968.

418.   Castro, Nei Leandro de. *Universo e vocabulário do* Grande Sertão. Rio de Janeiro: Olympio, 1970. xv + 195 pp.
Contains an introductory essay (3–24), followed by a comprehensive glossary of the vocabulary of *Grande sertão: Veredas*, with definitions of terms and quotations from the novel.

418a.   Vincent, Jon S. "Selected Bibliography." *João Guimarães Rosa.* Twayne World Authors Series 506. Boston: Twayne, 1978. 173–78.
Selected and annotated. Divided into primary sources and secondary sources.

Clarice Lispector

419.   Fitz, Earl E. "Bibliografía de y sobre Clarice Lispector." *Revista iberoamericana* 50 (1984): 293–304.
Contents: "Obras de Clarice Lispector," "Traduções," "Livros sobre Clarice

Lispector," "Artigos e ensaios em torno de Clarice Lispector."
Despite the Spanish title, the introduction is written in Portuguese.

419a.   ———. "Selected Bibliography." *Clarice Lispector.* Twayne World
         Authors Series 755. Boston: Twayne, 1985. 140–55.
         Divided into primary sources and secondary sources.

Pseudonyms

420. Menezes, Raimundo de. "Pseudônimos." *Dicionário literário brasileiro.*
      See no. 345.

421. Reis, Antônio Simões dos. *Pseudônimos brasileiros: Pequenos verbetes
      para um dicionário.* 6 vols. Rio de Janeiro: Valverde, 1941–43.
      Lists 997 pseudonyms used by Brazilian intellectuals. Each volume includes
      pseudonyms from A to Z and an index.

Stylistics

422. Hatzfeld, Helmut. *Bibliografía crítica de la nueva estilística aplicada a
      las literaturas románicas.* See no. 216.

423. ———. "Spain and Portugal." *A Critical Bibliography of the New Stylis-
      tics Applied to the Romance Literature 1900–1952.* See no. 217.

424. ———. "Portuguese and Luso-American Literature." *A Critical Bibliog-
      raphy of the New Stylistics Applied to the Romance Literature 1953–1965.*
      See no. 218

425. ———. "Stilische Studien in Portugal und Brasilien." See no. 219.

Bibliographies of Translations
General

426. *Index Translationum.* See no. 220.

427. *Yearbook of Comparative and General Literature.* See no. 221.

428. Sader, Marion. *Comprehensive Index to English Language Little Maga-
      zines 1890–1970.* See no. 222.

Latin America and Brazil

429. Berrien, William, John M. Fein, and Benjamin M. Woodbridge, Jr. "Brazilian Literature." [Rev. by Benjamin M. Woodbridge, Jr.] *The Romance Literatures. A Bibliography.* Vol. 3 of *The Literatures of the World in English Translation.* 3 vols. Ed. George B. Parks and Ruth Z. Temple. New York: Ungar, 1967–70. 3.1: 193–212.
A classified, annotated bibliography of works of and about Brazilian literature translated into English. Divided into: "Background," "Bibliography," "Literary Studies," "Collections," "Eighteenth and Nineteenth Centuries: Individual Authors," "Twentieth Century: Individual Authors."

430. Bryant, Solena V. *Brazil.* World Bibliographical Series 57. Oxford: Clio, 1985. 245 pp.
A classified, annotated bibliography. Includes a selective listing of Brazilian novels, poetry, and short stories in English translation. Index of authors, titles, and subjects.

431. Christensen, George K. "A Bibliography of Latin American Plays in English Translation." *Latin American Theatre Review* 6.2 (1973): 29–30.
Supplies data on both published and unpublished English translations of Latin American plays.

432. Freudenthal, Juan R., and Patricia M. Freudenthal. *Index to Anthologies of Latin American Literature in English Translation.* Boston: Hall, 1977. 199 pp.
Indexes works of Latin American literature in English translation appearing in some 120 books and journals. Does not include original Portuguese and Spanish titles.

433. Griffin, William J. "Brazilian Literature in English Translation." *Revista interamericana de bibliografía* 5 (1955): 21–37.
Contents: "Books and Pamphlets Containing Translations of Selected Items," "Poetry," "Novels," "Short Fiction," "Drama."
A bibliography of Brazilian literary works translated into English and published before 1954. Not annotated.

434. Hulet, Claude L. *Latin American Poetry in English Translation: A Bibliography.* Basic Bibliographies 2. Washington: Pan American Union, 1965. 182 pp.
Classified by country. Very thorough; normally includes original Portuguese or Spanish title.

435. ———. *Latin American Prose in English Translation: A Bibliography.* Basic Bibliographies 1. Washington: Pan American Union, 1964. 191 pp.
Arranged by genre and country.

436.   Johnson, Harvey L. "The Brazilian Mirror: Some Brazilian Writing in English Translation." *Americas: A Quarterly Review of Inter-American Cultural History* 21 (1965): 274–94.
A bibliographic essay on Brazilian literary and socio-historical works that were translated into English and published during the 1950s and the first half of the 1960s.

437.   Jones, Willis Knapp. *Latin American Writers in English Translation: A Classified Bibliography.* Detroit: Ethridge, 1972. vi + 140 pp.
A reprint of the 1944 edition. Contains brief sections on Brazilian poetry, drama, and fiction.

438.   Larsen, Jorgen Ingemann. *Bibliografi over latinamerikansk skonlitteratur pa dansk samt over danske bidrag til den latinamerikanske litteraturs historie.* 2 vols. Kobenhavn: n.p., 1982. 122 pp.
Organized by country; includes Brazil. Lists Latin American literature published in Danish translation between 1940 and 1979. Partially annotated. Includes an appendix of Latin American literature in Norwegian and Swedish translation (97–109).

439.   Levine, Suzanne Jill. *Latin American Fiction and Poetry in Translation.* New York: Center for Inter-American Relations, 1970. 72 pp.
Contents: "I. Anthologies," "II. Individual Works," "1. Poetry," "2. Fiction," "A. Short Stories," "B. Novels," "III. Indexes," "Authors," "Original Titles," "English Titles," "Countries."
Details the contents of 224 volumes.

440.   Mendes, Deoceli Regina Martins. "Les écrivains brésiliens traduits en France (1945–1975)." *Recherches et études comparatistes ibéro-françaises de la Sorbonne* 1 (1979): 57–60.

441.   Reichardt, Dieter. *Schöne Literatur lateinamerikanischer Autoren. Eine Übersicht der deutschen Übersetzungen mit biographischen Angaben.* Bibliographie un Dokumentation 6. Hamburg: Inst. für Iberoamerika-Kunde, 1965. 270 pp.
Indexes German translations of Latin American authors' works appearing as books or in anthologies; does not include those published in journals. Arranged by country.

442.   ———. *Lateinamerikanische Autoren: Literaturlexikon und Bibliographie der deutschen Übersetzungen.* Hamburg: Erdmann, 1972. 718 pp.
Includes a biobibliographical dictionary of Latin American authors (arranged by country) and a bibliography of German translations of Latin American authors' works published as books or in anthologies.

443.   Sarnacki, John. *Latin American Literature and History in Polish Translation: A Bibliography.* Port Huron: privately printed, 1973. ix + 84 pp.
Arranged by country. Includes studies of the authors and their works as well as reviews.

444.   Shaw, Bradley A. *Latin American Literature in English Translation: An Annotated Bibliography.* New York: New York UP, 1976. x + 144 pp.
Classified by genre and country. Indexes books and anthologies only. Includes a section on Brazilian literature (79–94).

445.   ———. *Latin American Literature in English 1975–1978.* Supp. to *Review: Latin American Literature and Arts* 24 (1979). 23 pp.
Lists and annotates 111 items; serves as an update and supplement to no. 444. Arranged alphabetically by author or editor. Divided into anthologies, individual works, additions to original volume (items published before 1975), and reprints (published before 1975).

446.   Siebenmann, Gustav, and Donatella Casetti. *Bibliographie der aus dem Spanischen, Portugiesischen, und Katalanischen ins Deutsche übersetzten Literatur (1945–1983).* See no. 226.

447.   Solver, Loretta. "Brazil and Portugal." *Women Writers in Translation: An Annotated Bibliography, 1945–82.* See no. 227.

448.   *Traduções de autores brasileiros e livros sobre o Brasil escritos em idioma estrangeiro.* Rio de Janeiro?: Ministério das Relações Exteriores, c. 1960. 92 pp.
Lists translations of Brazilian writers and books about Brazil written by foreigners in any of 18 languages.

449.   Woodbridge, Hensley C. "A Bibliography of Brazilian Poetry in English Translation: 1965–1977." *Luso-Brazilian Review* 15, supp. (1978): 161–88.
An attempt to update the information about Brazilian poetry in the Hulet poetry bibliography (no. 434). Arranged by poets' names. Includes a supplement.

Comparative Literature and Cross-Cultural Scholarship

General

450.   *Yearbook of Comparative and General Literature.* See no. 221.

Latin America and Brazil

451.   Musso Ambrosi, Luis Alberto. *Bibliografía uruguaya sobre Brasil.* See no. 24.

452.   Okinshevich, Leo. *Latin America in Soviet Writings: A Bibliography.* Ed. Robert G. Carlton. 2 vols. Baltimore: Johns Hopkins UP, 1966.
Vol. 1: xvii + 257 pp.; vol. 2: xii + 311 pp.

Includes sections on literary history, literary criticism, and translations of Latin American writers. Volume 1 deals with 1917–58; volume 2 covers 1959–64.

453.   Rogers, Francis M., and David T. Haberly. *Brazil, Portugal and Other Portuguese-Speaking Lands: A List of Books Primarily in English.* See no. 31.

454.   Sable, Martin H. *Latin American Studies in the Non-Western World and Eastern Europe: A Bibliography on Latin America in the Languages of Africa, Asia, the Middle East, and Eastern Europe, with Transliterations and Translations into English.* Metuchen: Scarecrow, 1970. xxiii + 701 pp.
Classified by country of publication. Lists 2,926 items on Latin American topics. Titles of studies are transliterated and translated into English. Excludes the Soviet Union because of the Okinshevich bibliography (no. 452). Author and subject indexes. Minimal coverage of literary works.

Bibliographies of Dissertations

United States

General

455.   *Microfilm Abstracts, Dissertation Abstracts, Dissertation Abstracts International.* See no. 232.

Hispanic and Luso-Brazilian

456.   Chatham, James R., and Enrique Ruiz-Fornells. *Dissertations in Hispanic Languages and Literatures: An Index of Dissertations Completed in the United States and Canada, 1876–1966.* See no. 233.

457.   Chatham, James R., and Carmen C. McClendon. *Dissertations in Hispanic Languages and Literatures: An Index of Dissertations Completed in the United States and Canada. Vol. 2, 1967–77.* See no. 234.

458.   Deal, Carl W. *Latin America and the Caribbean: A Dissertation Bibliography.* See no. 10.

459.   Hanson, Carl A. "Dissertations on Luso-Brazilian Topics. . . ." See no. 235.

460.   *Hispania.* See no. 236.

461.   *Modern Language Journal.* See no. 237.

462. "Recent Doctoral Dissertations." *Revista interamericana de bibliografía.* Beginning with 29.2 (1979), each issue includes a classified list of recent doctoral dissertations on Latin American topics.

Brazil

463. *Índice CENATE: Catálogo de teses universitárias.* São Paulo: Centro Nacional de Teses, Informações, Microformas e Sistemas, 1976– . A catalog of Brazilian university theses. Annual.

Western Europe

464. Chatham, James R., and Sara Matthews Scales. *Western European Dissertations on the Hispanic and Luso-Brazilian Languages and Literatures: A Retrospective Index.* See no. 240.

France

465. Fichier Central des Thèses. See no. 241.

466. "Liste alphabétique des thèses de troisième cycle soutenus en France en 1980 (toute discipline)." *Cahiers du monde hispanique et luso-brésilien* 37 (1981): 256–66; also for 1981, 39 (1982): 175–83.
Includes French theses on all aspects of Latin America. Contains some abstracts.

Germany and Austria

467. Flasche, Hans. *Romance Languages and Literature as Presented in German Doctoral Dissertations, 1885–1950.* See no. 242.

468. Janik, Dieter. "Tesis de habilitación y tesis de doctorado realizadas en las universidades de la República Federal de Alemania, de la República Democrática Alemana y de Austria sobre temas de lengua y literatura hispanoamericanas y brasileñas (1945–1979)." *Iberoromania* ns 5 (1976 [pub. 1980]): 225–35.
Divided into "Tesis de habilitación" and "Tesis de doctorado."

469. "Die romanistischen Dissertationen." *Romanistisches Jahrbuch.* See no. 244.

United Kingdom and Ireland

470.   Jones, C. A. "Theses in Hispanic Studies Approved for Higher Degrees by British Universities to 1971." See no. 245.

471.   Hodcroft, F. W. "Theses in Hispanic Studies Approved for Higher Degrees by British and Irish Universities (1972–1974)." See no. 246.

472.   MacKenzie, D. "Theses in Hispanic Studies Approved for Higher Degrees by British and Irish Universities (1975–1978)." See no. 247.

473.   Johnson, M. "Theses in Hispanic Studies Approved for Higher Degrees by British and Irish Universities (1979–1982)." See no. 248.

National Bibliographies

General Bibliographical Studies

474.   Woodbridge, Hensley C. "Latin American National Bibliography." *Encyclopedia of Library and Information Science.* Ed. Allen Kent. Vol. 36. New York: Dekker, 1983. 271–343. 42 vols. 1968–87.
A bibliographical essay, the most extensive on Latin American national bibliography to date. Includes items pertaining to Brazil (287–90).

475.   Zimmerman, Irene. *Current National Bibliographies of Latin America: A State of the Art Study.* Gainesville: U of Florida, Center for Latin American Studies, 1971. x + 139 pp.
A critical study of the publication of current national bibliographies by Latin American countries.

Brazilian Bibliographies

476.   *Anuário brasileiro de literatura.* 8 vols. (1937–44). Rio de Janeiro: Pongetti, 1937–44.
Each volume includes a classified list of the literary works published in Brazil during the previous year. The volume for 1943–44 was published by Valverde.

477.   *Anuário da literatura brasileira.* Rio de Janeiro, 1960–63.
Each volume includes a bibliography of the literary works published in Brazil during the previous year.

478.   *BBB: Boletim bibliográfico brasileiro.* Rio de Janeiro: Estante, 1952–67.
A classified monthly bibliography, sponsored by the União Brasileira de Escritores, of the books published in Brazil. Index. Does not include serial publications.

479.   *Bibliografia brasileira.* Rio de Janeiro: Inst. Nacional do Livro, 1938–55; 1963–66.
A classified current bibliography. Arranged according to authors' names, titles, and subjects. Continues in the *Revista do livro* (no. 485) and the *Bibliografia brasileira mensal* (no. 480).

480.   *Bibliografia brasileira mensal.* Rio de Janeiro: Inst. Nacional do Livro, Nov. 1967–Apr. 1972.
A classified current bibliography. A continuation of the *Bibliografia brasileira* (no. 479) and the *Revista do livro* (no. 485). Annual index as of 1971.

481.   Biblioteca Municipal Mário de Andrade. *Boletim bibliográfico.* São Paulo, 197?– .
A continuation of no. 482.

482.   Biblioteca Pública Municipal de São Paulo. *Boletim bibliográfico.* São Paulo, 1943– .
Each issue contains, in addition to articles, the "Registro bibliográfico." Starting with volume 24, the name of the library appears as "Biblioteca Municipal Mário de Andrade." See also no. 481.

483.   *Boletim internacional de bibliografia luso-brasileira.* See no. 250.

484.   *Livros novos. Current Books. Neuerscheinungen.* Ed. J. Heydecker. São Paulo: Atlantis, 1972– .
A monthly classified bibliography of Brazilian publications.

485.   *Revista do livro.* Rio de Janeiro: Inst. Nacional do Livro, 1956–70.
Includes a classified current bibliography through 1965. A continuation of the *Bibliografia brasileira* (no. 479).

486.   Rio de Janeiro. Biblioteca Nacional. *Boletim bibliográfico da Biblioteca Nacional.* ns. 1951– .
Irregular. The old series began in 1918 and lasted until 1938. A classified current bibliography. "A partir de 1976, processado por computador."

Union Lists and Library and Collection Catalogs

General

United States

487.   *Library of Congress Catalog.* See no. 255.

488.   *The National Union Catalog.* See nos. 256–57.

489.   *Union List of Serials in Libraries of the United States and Canada.* See no. 258.

490.   *New Serials Titles: A Union List of Serials Commencing Publication after December 31, 1949.* . . . See no. 259.

France

491.   Bibliothèque Nationale. *Catalogue général des livres imprimés.* See nos. 260-62.

492.   ———. Département des Périodiques. *Catalogue collectif des périodiques du début du xviiième siècle à 1939.* See no. 263.

Spain

493.   Madrid. Ministerio de Cultura. Dirección General de Libro y Biblioteca. *Catálogo colectivo de publicaciones periódicas en bibliotecas españolas.* See no. 264.

United Kingdom

494.   British Museum. *General Catalog of Printed Books.* . . . See nos. 265-66.

495.   *British Union-Catalog of Periodicals.* . . . See no. 267.

Latin America and Brazil

United States

Library of Congress

496.   Library of Congress. *Accessions List: Brazil—Cumulative List of Serials.* 1975- .
A monthly bibliographical listing of the Brazilian publications acquired by the Library of Congress. Not limited to literature. Entries are classified into broad sections: "Monographs" and "Serial Publications."

497.   Jackson, William Vernon. *Catalog of Brazilian Acquisitions of the Library of Congress, 1964-1974.* Boston: Hall, 1976. xvii + 751 pp.
A classified bibliography of the Brazilian acquisitions of the Library of Congress (1964-74). Includes a section on languages and literature (375-482).

General

498.   Charno, Steven M. *Latin American Newspapers in the United States: A Union List.* Austin: U of Texas P, 1978. xiv + 619 pp.
Lists the Latin American newspaper holdings of 70 US libraries.

499.   Downs, Robert B. "Spanish, Portuguese and Latin American Literature." See nos. 268–71.

500.   Fernández, Oscar. *A Preliminary Listing of Foreign Periodical Holdings in the United States and Canada Which Give Coverage to Portuguese and Brazilian Language and Literature.* See no. 13.

501.   Mesa, Rosa Quintero. *Latin American Serial Documents. A Holdings List. V. 2: Brazil.* Ann Arbor: UMI, 1968. viii + 343 + 12 pp.
An inventory of the Brazilian serial documents found in US libraries.

502.   Nelson, Bonnie E. "Spain, Portugal, Latin America and the Caribbean." See no. 273.

Specific Libraries and Collections

503.   Catholic University of America. *Oliveira Lima Library.* See no. 274.

504.   University of Florida, Gainesville, Libraries. *Catalog of the Latin American Collection.* 13 vols. Boston: Hall, 1973; 1st supp. 7 vols. 1979.
A reproduction of the card catalog; lists some 210,000 items.

505.   Hispanic Society of America. *Catalog of the Library.* See no. 275.

506.   Gillett, Theresa, and Helen McIntyre. *Catalog of Luso-Brazilian Material in the University of New Mexico Libraries.* See no. 15.

507.   University of Texas Library. *Catalog of the Latin American Collection.* 31 vols. Boston: Hall, 1969; 1st supp. 5 vols. 1971; 2nd supp. 3 vols. 1973; 3rd supp. 8 vols. 1975; 4th supp. 3 vols. 1977.
A catalog of one of the largest Latin American collections in the United States. Includes some 175,000 items (books, pamphlets, journals, newspapers, microfilm).

508.   *Bibliographic Guide to Latin American Studies, 1979– .* Boston: Hall, 1980– .
The annual supplement to the University of Texas catalog.

509.   Tulane University Library. *Catalog of the Latin American Library of the Tulane University Library, New Orleans.* 10 vols. Boston: Hall, 1970; 1st supp. 2 vols. 1973; 2nd supp. 2 vols. 1975; 3rd supp. 2 vols. 1978.
A catalog of the Latin American collection, with special emphasis on Mexico and Central America.

Brazil

510. *Catálogo da Biblioteca de Rui Barbosa.* Rio de Janeiro: Ministério da
Educação e Saúde, Casa de Rui Barbosa, 1944-   .
Vol. 1 (A–B): [1944], lxxii + 411 pp.; vol. 2 (C–E): [1951], 465 pp.; vol. 3 (F–H):
[1957], 346 pp.
A catalog of the large personal library left by Rui Barbosa.

511. Rio de Janeiro. Biblioteca Nacional. *Periódicos brasileiros em
microformas: Catálogo coletivo.* Rio de Janeiro: Biblioteca Nacional,
1981. 296 pp.
A bibliography of the microforms of Brazilian journals and newspapers found
in the libraries of several countries. Preliminary editions were published in 1976
and 1979.

Germany

512. Berlin. Ibero-Amerikanisches Institut. *Schlagwortkatalog des Ibero-
Amerikanischen Instituts.* . . . See no. 279.

Netherlands

513. Bibliotheek der Rijksuniversiteit te Utrecht. *Portugal e o Brasil:
Catálogo.* . . . See no. 280.

United Kingdom

514. Luso-Brazilian Council. London. *Canning House Library.* . . . See no.
281.

Bibliographies of Bibliographies

General

515. *Bibliographische Berichte.* See no. 282.

Latin America and Brazil

516. Basseches, Bruno. *Bibliography of Brazilian Bibliographies. Uma bibliografia das bibliografias brasileiras.* Detroit: Ethridge, 1978. 185 pp.
Alphabetically arranged; not classified. Index.

517.   Bryant, Shasta M. *Selective Bibliography of Bibliographies of Hispanic American Literature.* 2nd ed., rev. and enl. Austin: U of Texas, Inst. of Latin American Studies, 1976. x + 100 pp.
First edition, Washington: Pan American Union, 1966. An annotated, selective bibliography of the major bibliographies of Spanish American and Brazilian literature. Author index.

518.   Geohegan, Abel Rodolfo. *Obras de referencia de América Latina.* See no. 14.

519.   Gropp, Arthur E. *A Bibliography of Latin American Bibliographies.* Metuchen: Scarecrow, 1968. ix + 515 pp.

520.   ———. *A Bibliography of Latin American Bibliographies: Supplement.* Metuchen: Scarecrow, 1971. xiii + 277 pp.

521.   ———. *Latin American Bibliographies Published in Periodicals.* 2 vols. Metuchen: Scarecrow, 1976.

The Gropp bibliographies (nos. 519–21) are all classified. Nos. 522–24 supplement Gropp.

522.   Cordeiro, Daniel Raposo. *A Bibliography of Latin American Bibliographies: Social Sciences and Humanities.* Metuchen: Scarecrow, 1979. vii + 272 pp.

523.   Piedracueva, Haydée. *A Bibliography of Latin American Bibliographies, 1957-1979: Humanities and Social Sciences.* Metuchen: Scarecrow, 1982. 329 pp.

524.   Seminar on the Acquisition of Latin American Library Materials. "Annual Report on Latin American and Caribbean Bibliographic Activities." Working Paper.
An unannotated, classified bibliography of bibliographies is among the working papers issued by SALALM each year after its annual meeting. The title, compiler, and other data vary. Lists book-length bibliographies as well as those published in journals. Often included are such categories as national bibliographies, personal bibliographies, bibliographies on language and literature, and bibliographies compiled as theses and dissertations. Supplements the bibliographies of Gropp (nos. 519–21), Cordeiro (no. 522), and Piedracueva (no. 523).

525.   Peraza Sarausa, Fermín. *Bibliografías corrientes de la América Latina.* Medellín: Anuario Bibliográfico Cubano (en Colombia), 1962. vi + 46 pp.
Contents: "América Latina (generales, especiales)," "Bibliografías nacionales (por país)," "Índice analítico."
Contains 148 entries. Editions were also published in 1964, 1965, 1966, and 1969. The 1969 edition includes 236 titles. Place of publication varies; the most recent editions were published in Florida.

526.   Reis, Antônio Simões dos. *Bibliografia das bibliografias brasileiras*. Rio de Janeiro: Inst. Nacional do Livro, 1942. viii + 186 pp.
Works listed are arranged by year (1741–1941). Author and subject indexes.

527.   Woods, Richard D. *Reference Materials on Latin America in English: The Humanities*. Metuchen: Scarecrow, 1980. xii + 639 pp.
An annotated, critical, alphabetically arranged bibliography of 1,252 reference works on Latin American topics published in English.

528.   Zubatsky, David S. "Annotated Bibliography of Latin American Author Bibliographies. Part IV: Brazil." *Chasqui* 7.1 (1977): 35–54.
An annotated bibliography; classified by authors. Opens with a section on general bibliographies. Lists 57 titles.

529.   ———. *Latin American Literary Authors: An Annotated Guide to Bibliographies*. Metuchen: Scarecrow, 1986. ix + 332 pp.
Includes and updates material from no. 528, listing author bibliographies that appear in periodicals, books, dissertations, and festschriften. Alphabetical by author, followed by a listing of general bibliographies and biobibliographies. No index.

*Luso-African and
Other Lusophone Literatures*

Bibliographies and Other Reference Works: Lusophone Africa

530. Bender, Gerald J., et al. *Portugal in Africa: A Bibliography of the UCLA Collection.* Los Angeles: U of California, African Studies Center, 1972. xxiii + 315 pp.
A classified bibliography. Includes a section on the university's Luso-African literary holdings (177–90).

531. César, Amândio, and Mário António. *Elementos para uma bibliografia da literatura portuguesa ultramarina contemporânea: Poesia. ficção. memorialismo. ensaio.* Lisboa: Agência Geral do Ultramar, 1968. 177 pp.
A classified bibliography; classification by territory. Arranged by author within each geographical category.

532. Collemacine, Joan E. "A Select Bibliography of Contemporary African Poetry in the Portuguese Language." *Africa* [Rome] 31.3 (1976): 445–47.
Divided into: "Bibliographies," "Original Texts in Portuguese," "Studies, Critiques," "Other Language Editions."

533. *Encyclopedia of World Literature in the Twentieth Century.* See no. 167.

534. McCarthy, Joseph M. *Guinea-Bissau and Cape Verde Islands: A Comprehensive Bibliography.* New York: Garland, 1977. 196 pp.
A classified bibliography. Includes sections on language (117–20) and literature (143–67).

535. Moser, Gerald M. *A Tentative Portuguese-African Bibliography: Portuguese Literature in Africa and African Literature in the Portuguese Language.* University Park: Pennsylvania State U Libraries, 1970. xi + 151 pp.
Divided into: "Folk Literature," "Art Literature (Essays, Novels, Poems, Stories, Theater)," "History and Criticism of Literature (Anthologies, Bibliographies, Histories of Literature, Literary Criticism, Literary Theory)."
The third section is limited to studies written by Portuguese and Afro-

Portuguese authors. Index of authors, with biographical notes. There is also a short supplement.

536.   Moser, Gerald M., and Manuel Ferreira. *Bibliografia das literaturas africanas de expressão portuguesa.* Lisboa: Nacional; Moeda, 1983. 407 pp.
Updates no. 535 through 1979. Adds a section on literary periodicals of Portuguese-speaking Africa. Includes an index of authors, works, and journals.

537.   Zubatsky, David S. *A Guide to Resources in United States Libraries and Archives for the Study of Cape Verdes, Guinea (Bissau), São Tomé-Príncipe, Angola and Mozambique.* Essays in Portuguese Studies 1. Durham: International Conference Group on Modern Portugal, 1977. 29 pp.
A brief guide to some US libraries with holdings that relate to Luso-African studies.

Bibliography: Portuguese in the United States

538.   Pap, Leo. *The Portuguese in the United States: A Bibliography.* New York: Center for Migration Studies, 1976. x + 80 pp.
Includes a section listing works of fiction that portray Portuguese immigrants to the United States (55–60). Not annotated.

Index of Authors, Editors, and Compilers

Abreu, Maria Isabel, 342
Aguiar, Thereza da Silva, 366
Albuquerque, Paulo de Medeiros, 211
Almeida, Átila Augusto F. de, 352
Almeida, Horácio de, 1, 128
Alves, Afonso Telles, 60
Alves, Henrique L., 381
Amaral, Amadeu, 121
Amaral, Eloy do, 208
Angenot, Jean-Pierre, 100
Anjos, Margarida dos, 64
António, Mário, 531
Aranha, Brito, 173
Armistead, Samuel G., 184
Aulete, Francisco Júlio Caldas, 57
Avery, Catherine B., 80
Azevedo, Francisco Ferreira dos Santos, 75
Azevedo, Luísa Maria de Castro, 189

Bach, Kathryn F., 2
Bagby Júnior, Alberto I., 399
Baldensperger, Fernand, 228
Barrau-Dihigo, L., 283
Basseches, Bruno, 516
Batalha, Graciete Nogueira, 143
Batista, Sebastião Nunes Hugolino de Sena, 403
Beaurepaire-Rohan, 101
Becco, Horacio Jorge, 303–04
Bédé, Jean-Albert, 164
Bender, Gerald J., 530
Berrien, William, 23, 223, 429
Bittencourt, Adalzira, 383
Blakemore, Harold, 335
Blanco, José, 213
Boléo, Manuel Paiva, 26, 84
Brasil, Assis, 305, 333
Brinches, Victor, 162, 334
Bryant, Shasta M., 517
Bryant, Solena V., 430
Bueno, Francisco da Silveira, 44

Cabral, António, 144
Cabral, Tomé, 129

Callage, Roque, 127
Câmara, Joaquim Mattoso, Jr., 5
Campos, Geir, 331
Campos, J. L. de, 66
Cardoso Júnior, 72
Cardote, Fernando, 97
Carlton, Robert G., 452
Carmo, Célio Assis do, 173, 351
Carmo, Pinto do, 364
Carneiro, Édison, 130
Carpeaux, Otto Maria, 305
Carpenter, Charles A., 360
Carvalho, J., 58
Cascudo, Luís da Câmara, 102
Casetti, Donatella, 226, 446
Castro, Nei Leandro de, 418
Catalán, Diego, 184
Catton, Albano Pereira, 212
César, Amândio, 531
Chamberlain, Bobby J., 17, 103, 306, 309, 313
Charno, Steven M., 498
Chatham, James R., 233–34, 238, 240–41, 456–57, 464
Christensen, George K., 431
Cintra, Maria Adelaide Valle, 178
Cisneros, Luis Jaime, 304
Clarke, Edna Jansen de Mello, 80
Clerot, L. F. R., 131
Cochofel, João José, 163
Coelho, Jacinto do Prado, 165, 336
Coelho, Nelly Novaes, 372
Coelho Neto, Paulo, 404
Collemacine, Joan E., 532
Collier, Simon, 335
Cordeiro, Daniel Raposo, 522
Corrêa, Piaguaçu, 126
Corrêa, Romaguera, 127
Coruja, Antônio Álvares Pereira, 127
Costa, Agenor, 76
Costa, Alexandre de Carvalho, 91
Costa, F. A. Pereira da, 132
Cunha, A. G., 198
Cunha, Antônio, 408
Cunha, Antônio Geraldo da, 45, 50
Curran, Mark J., 354

Da Cal, Ernesto Guerra, 207
Dalgado, Sebastião Rodolfo, 54
Deal, Carl W., 10, 458
de Gorog, Ralph Paul, 11
Delgado, Manuel Joaquim, 92
Dias, Jaime Lopes, 93
Dietrich, Wolf, 12
Downs, Robert B., 268–71, 499
Doyle, Plínio, 417

Edgerton, William B., 164
Elkins, A. C., Jr., 203, 388
Estorninho, Carlos, 224
Eulálio, Alexandre, 348

Fein, John M., 429
Felgueiras, A., 206
Fernandes, Francisco, 62–63, 77
Fernández, Oscar, 13, 272, 500
Ferre, Pedro, 171
Ferreira, Aurélio Buarque de Holanda, 64–65
Ferreira, Herti Hoeppner, 156
Ferreira, Manuel, 536
Ferreira, Marina Baird, 64
Fischer, Jango, 348
Fitz, Earl E., 419–19a
Fiúza, Mário, 53
Flasche, Hans, 242, 467
Fonseca, Martinho Augusto Ferreira da, 173
Ford, Jeremiah Denis Matthias, 307
Forstner, L. S., 203
Foster, David W., 154, 308, 340, 380
Foster, Virginia Ramos, 380
Foulché-Delbosc, Raymond, 283
Franco, Cid, 104
Fraser, Howard M., 236
Freire, Laudelino, 66
Freudenthal, Juan R., 432
Freudenthal, Patricia M., 432
Friedrich, Werner P., 228

Galvão, José, 214
Garcia, Hamílcar, 57
Garlant, Julia, 300
Geohegan, Abel Rodolfo, 14, 518
Gillett, Theresa, 15, 278, 506
Girão, Raimundo, 133
Golden, Herbert H., 16, 155
Goldsmith, V. F., 193

Gomes, Celeuta Moreira, 365–66
Gomes, Suelí Guimarães, 45
Green, John N., 25
Griffin, William J., 433
Gropp, Arthur E., 519–21
Guérios, Rosário Farani Mansur, 67, 85
Guimarães, F. Marques, 62–63
Guimarães, Júlio César Castañon, 45
Gusmão, F. A. Rodrigues de, 179
Gyberg, Erik, 230

Haberly, David T., 31, 231, 453
Hallewell, Laurence, 300
Hammond, Muriel E., 267, 495
Hanson, Carl A., 235, 459
Harmon, Ronald M., 17, 103, 309
Hatzfeld, Helmut, 216–19, 422–25
Heydecker, J., 484
Hodcroft, F. W., 246, 471
Hoffman, Herbert H., 358–59
Hoge, Henry W., 18
Horch, Hans Jürgen W., 392
Horch, Rosemarie Erika, 195, 202
Horn-Monval, Madeleine, 225
Houaiss, Antônio, 68, 79–80, 87
Hower, Alfred, 223
Hulet, Claude L., 434–35

Iannone, Carlos Alberto, 215

Jackson, William Vernon, 19, 301, 497
Jacquemin, Jean-Pierre, 100
Janik, Dieter, 468
Johnson, Harvey L., 436
Johnson, M., 248, 473
Jones, C. A., 245, 470
Jones, Willis Knapp, 437

Klein, Leonard S., 167, 339, 341, 533

Lapa, Albino, 94
Lapa, Manuel Rodrigues, 186
Larsen, Jorgen Ingemann, 438
Lauerhass, Ludwig, Jr., 302
Leão, Múcio, 390, 394
Leite, Serafim, 387
Lello, Edgar, 61
Lello, José, 61
Levine, Suzanne Jill, 439

Lima, Henrique de Campos Ferreira, 204
Lincoln, Joseph Newhall, 343
Livermore, H. V., 224
Lohman Villena, Guillermo, 304
Lombardi, Mary, 310
Lorenzo, Ramón, 47
Luft, Celso Pedro, 77, 168, 344
Luz, João Baptista da, 65
Lyday, Leon F., 360
Lyon, Ted, 311

Macedo, Neusa Dias, 156
MacGregor-Villarreal, Mary, 370
Machado, Álvaro Manuel, 171
Machado, Diogo Barbosa, 179
Machado, José Pedro, 46, 72
Mackenzie, D., 247, 472
Magalhães, Álvaro, 69
Magalhães Júnior, Raymundo, 105
Magne, Augusto, 52, 187
Maia, Pedro Américo, 367
Manuppella, Giacinto, 20
Marques, Joaquim Campelo, 64
Marroni, Giovanna, 185
Martha, M. Cardoso, 208
Martin, Priscilla Clark, 82
Martins, António Coimbra, 196
Martins, Ari, 377
Massa, Jean-Michel, 398
McCarthy, Joseph M., 534
McClendon, Carmen C., 234, 238, 457
McIntyre, Helen, 15, 278, 506
Megenney, William W., 106
Melo, Luís Correa de, 379
Mendes, Amando, 140
Mendes, Deoceli Regina Martins, 440
Mendonça, Renato, 107
Menezes, Raimundo de, 345, 420
Mesa, Rosa Quintero, 501
Mesquita, Esmeralda Ribeiro de, 197
Messner, Dieter, 51
Miranda, Vicente Chermont de, 141
Moisés, Massaud, 156, 169, 313, 332, 347
Moraes, Jomar, 375
Moraes, Luiz Carlos de, 127
Moraes, Rubens Borba de, 23, 314, 385-86
Moreno, Augusto, 72
Morna, Maria de Fátima, 171
Moser, Gerald M., 223, 315, 535-36
Mota, Mauro, 108
Moutinho, Stella Rodrigo Octávio, 64
Musso Ambrosi, Luis Alberto, 24, 451

Naro, Anthony M., 25
Nascentes, Antenor, 48-49, 55, 78, 86, 109-10, 122
Nascentes, Olavo Aníbal, 78
Nelson, Bonnie E., 273, 502
Nobre, Eduardo, 95-96
Nogueira, Júlio, 199
Nonato, Raimundo, 134
Nunes, Maria Luisa, 316, 405

Ocampo de Gómez, Aurora M., 346
Okinshevich, Leo, 452
Olteanu, Tudora Sandru, 83
Ortega, Julio, 304
Ortêncio, Waldomiro Bariani, 142
Osório, João de Castro, 170

Paes, José Paulo, 347
Palhano, Herbert, 188
Palls, Terry L., 313
Pap, Leo, 538
Parks, George B., 223, 429
Passetti, Manuel, 97
Passos, Alexandre, 135
Pati, Francisco, 400
Pederneiras, Raul, 123
Peixoto, Vicente, 58
Pellegrini, Silvio, 185
Peraza Sarausa, Fermín, 525
Perdigão, Edmylson, 124
Pereira, Benjamim Enes, 27, 174
Piedracueva, Haydée, 523
Pietzschke, Fritz, 81
Pinto, Gilda da Costa, 45
Placer, Xavier, 406
Pontes, Joel, 111
Pontes, Maria de Lourdes, 201
Porter, Dorothy B., 28, 382
Posner, Rebecca, 25
Prado, José E. A. do, 80
Price, Glanville, 2
Primus, Wilma J., 29
Pugliesi, Márcio, 112
Py, Fernando, 412

Quadros, Jânio, 71

Ramos, F. J. da Silva, 58
Raphael, Maxwell I., 307

Rebello, Luiz Francisco, 175
Rebelo, Marques, 389
Rector, Mônica, 113
Reichardt, Dieter, 441–42
Reinecke, John E., 30
Reis, Antônio Simões dos, 209, 318–19, 356, 395, 421, 526
Reis, Irene Monteiro, 401
Reis, J. E. Morgado, 176
Reis, Roberto, 340
Rela, Walter, 313, 361
Révah, I. S., 176
Ribeiro Filho, João de Souza, 376
Rodríguez Richart, José, 243
Rogers, Francis M., 31, 231, 453
Rohlfs, Gerhard, 32
Rosa, Ubiratan, 58, 71
Ruiz-Fornells, Enrique, 233, 456

Sá, Victor de, 210
Sable, Martin H., 320, 454
Sacramento Blake, Augusto Victorino Alves, 348
Sader, Marion, 222, 428
Saenger, Erwin, 267, 495
Salles, Diva de Oliveira, 45
Sánchez, Luis Alberto, 321
Sánchez Romeralo, Antonio, 184
Sant'Ana, Moacir Medeiros de, 410
Santiago, Paulino, 136
Santos, Eduardo dos, 97
Sarnacki, John, 443
Scales, Sara Matthews, 240, 464
Schmidt-Radefeldt, Jürgen, 34
Séguier, Jaime de, 61
Sequeira, F. J. Martins, 98
Seraine, Florival, 137
Seymour-Smith, Martin, 172, 349
Sharrer, Harvey L., 183
Shaw, Bradley A., 444–45
Shimose, Pedro, 166, 337
Siebenmann, Gustav, 226, 446
Silva, Adalberto Prado e, 70
Silva, António de Morais, 72
Silva, Braz da, 114
Silva, Euclides Carneiro da, 115–16
Silva, Felisbelo da, 117
Silva, Padre Fernando Augusto da, 145
Silva, Giovani Mafra e, 64
Silva, Inocêncio Francisco da, 173, 350
Silva, J. A. Capela e, 99
Silveira, Alarico, 89
Simches, Seymour O., 16, 155

Skidmore, Thomas E., 335
Sletsjøe, Leif, 35
Soares, Antônio Joaquim de Macedo, 73
Soares, Ernesto, 173
Soares, Julião Rangel de Macedo, 73
Sobrinho, Cláudio Mello, 45
Sobrinho, José Alves, 352
Sodré, Nelson Werneck, 36, 322
Solé, Carlos A., 342
Solver, Loretta, 227, 447
Sousa, José Galante de, 323–24, 363, 396–97
Souto Maior, Mário, 118–19
Souza, José Soares de, 173
Spalding, Walter, 127
Stathatos, Constantine Christopher, 191
Stern, Irwin, 338
Stewart, James D., 267, 495

Tacla, Ariel, 125
Tate, R. Brian, 239
Tavani, Giuseppe, 180
Tavares, Paulo, 414–15
Taylor, James L., 82
Temple, Ruth Z., 223, 429
Titus, Edna Brown, 258, 489
Topete, José Manuel, 325
Trigueiros, Edilberto, 138

Valis, Noël, 37, 157, 326
Velho Sobrinho, J. F., 351
Venâncio Filho, Francisco, 402
Verdelho, Telmo, 200
Vianna, Fernando Antônio de Mello, 80
Vieira [de Mello], Antenor, 90
Vieira, Yara Frateschi, 156
Vieira Filho, Domingos, 139
Villas-Boas, Pedro, 378
Vincent, Jon S., 418a
Vincke, Jacques L., 100
Viotti, Manuel, 120
Viterbo, Fr. Joaquim de Santa Rosa de, 53

Welsh, Doris Varner, 277
Whitten, Arthur F., 307
Wilgus, A. Curtis, 158, 327
Williams, Harry F., 38, 181
Woodbridge, Benjamin M., Jr., 223, 429
Woodbridge, Hensley C., 449, 474
Woods, Richard D., 527
Woodyard, George, 360

Zeitlin, Marion A., 223
Zimmerman, Irene, 475
Zubatsky, David S., 40–43, 159–61, 284,
  328–30, 528–29, 537
Zúquete, Afonso, 74